a prime resource, not only for the church in Myanmar but also for similar circumstances, where the church is endeavoring to live out the ministry of reconciliation as Christ's ambassadors. I would also like to thank van Dorp from the bottom of my heart for choosing Myanmar as the focus of his brilliant research as we struggle for "sustainable peace."

Saw Mya Min Lwin
Associate Pastor, Christ's Church (Ahlone), Myanmar

I warmly welcome this book, as it displays van Dorp's ardent desire to see the church in Myanmar radiate a sound, biblical ecclesiology that brings reconciliation to the whole of society and makes it possible for the church to grow among all peoples. Toward this end, it overviews Myanmar's historical, religious, and ethnic context to demonstrate their influence on the current national situation and discusses the impact of local and international politics, along with interethnic relations, upon the church's development. Biblical teaching about humility and reconciliation is examined and applied to express the hope that people will unite in their worship of Christ, walls of separation will be broken down, and the majority population will open up to the truths of the gospel. Christian workers in Myanmar and other countries with disparate population groups will benefit from the biblical and practical wisdom found here.

Walter McConnell, PhD
Head of Mission Research,
OMF International, UK

Arend van Dorp explores a biblical understanding of the church and develops an inclusive model of missional church. This book will stimulate, energize, and propel missional Christian leaders in Myanmar to rethink, reform, and renew a biblical ecclesiology. It is a must-read for all who want to be empowered to bring real and lasting change.

Peter Thein Nyunt, PhD
Director,
Theological Commission of Myanmar Evangelical Christian Alliance

In the midst of the brokenness and suffering of the world, the church exists as a community of reconciliation. Or at least it should. In *Ethnic Diversity and Reconciliation*, Arend van Dorp explores the complexities facing the church in Myanmar in becoming a more inclusive, multiethnic fellowship that embodies the gospel of reconciliation within the church and wider society. Van Dorp's work will be an excellent resource, not just for the church in Myanmar, but for all contexts where the church is seeking to live out its missional calling as a peacemaker.

Peter Rowan, PhD
Co-National Director,
OMF International, UK

This is a book that all Myanmar Christian mission practitioners need to read. Delving beneath the surface, it explores the biblical perspective of the church and develops an inclusive model of the missional church in Myanmar.

Stephen Vum Cung Nung, PhD
Head of Intercultural Studies Department, Director of DMin Program,
Myanmar Evangelical Graduate School of Theology

A remarkable work in many ways. Van Dorp first puts together a cogent analysis of the problem of fragmentation and division in the Myanmar church and wider society. Following this, he constructs an elegant formulation of scriptural and theological themes relevant to diversity and reconciliation. He cleverly balances these two, noting that a church existing in the image of a triune God must present unity in diversity to a country in need. While drawing on literature from the West, van Dorp is careful to take account of his particular context. Finally, the book moves into a series of useful and practical proposals for ministry. This book has the potential to bring genuine and meaningful change to the church and help it serve a suffering nation as salt and light. This essential method and message will surely have application around the world.

Paul Woods, PhD
Research Tutor, East Asian Theology and Contextual Theology,
Oxford Centre for Mission Studies, UK

Arend van Dorp has researched on the history and the present context of multiethnic churches in Myanmar. He fully understands the issues and the solution of what needs to be done for multiethnic churches toward reconciliation according to biblical perspective. This is a book like a window into the present and the future development of churches in Myanmar.

Salai Yaw Han, DMin
Principal, Stars of Dawn Wholistic Leadership Institute
General Secretary, Myanmar Christ's Mission Cooperation Board

As we are facing pandemic, conflict, the climate crisis, inequities, brokenness, and suffering today, the church, the assembly of God's covenant people, should endure as a community of reconciliation. In this book, Arend van Dorp investigates the challenges that the church in Myanmar face as it becomes a more embracing multiethnic community, focusing on reconciliation both within the church and wider society. I commend van Dorp's labour, which will be

Global Perspectives Series

Ethnic Diversity and Reconciliation

Langham

GLOBAL LIBRARY

Ethnic Diversity and Reconciliation

A Missional Model for the Church in Myanmar

Arend van Dorp

Langham

GLOBAL LIBRARY

© 2022 Arend van Dorp

Published 2022 by Langham Global Library
An imprint of Langham Publishing
www.langhampublishing.org

Langham Publishing and its imprints are a ministry of Langham Partnership

Langham Partnership
PO Box 296, Carlisle, Cumbria, CA3 9WZ, UK
www.langham.org

ISBNs:
978-1-83973-650-6 Print
978-1-83973-715-2 ePub
978-1-83973-716-9 Mobi
978-1-83973-717-6 PDF

British Library Cataloguing-in-Publication Data
A catalogue record for this book is available from the British Library

ISBN: 978-1-83973-650-6

Cover & Book Design: projectluz.com

Contents

Acknowledgments

I would like to thank my OMF leaders for allowing me to engage in the Doctor of Ministry program at Fuller Theological Seminary, and for the support I received from them during this time. I am also grateful to my colleagues for their understanding during the times when I was less accessible to them because of my studies. To my fellow students in the Ministry and Leadership in Asian Contexts cohort, I enjoyed the journey together with you and I will miss you. Furthermore, I would like to express my deep appreciation to those Myanmar Christian leaders who, while remaining anonymous, agreed to be interviewed by me. Their insights and comments significantly deepened my understanding of the challenging conditions encountered by the church in Myanmar. Finally, I thank the Myanmar Christians: your faith and perseverance were an inspiration to me during the six years I had the privilege of living in your country.

Introduction

Missionary work in Myanmar has seen only limited response among the Bamar (ethnic Burmese) people, while the Karen and other minorities throughout the nation have shown much greater openness and receptivity.[1] Thus, the churches in Myanmar are overwhelmingly made up of people from ethnic minorities. Moreover, many churches are ethnoculturally delineated and predominantly consist of a single ethnic group. This ethnolinguistic demarcation between Myanmar churches creates a significant obstacle for those who exist outside these ethnolinguistic groups and wish to join.[2] It also clashes with an understanding of the church as a universal body of believers from diverse ethnic, social, and cultural backgrounds.

This cultural makeup of many churches makes it extremely difficult for Bamar converts to integrate into a church. Whereas in the larger society they occupy a dominant and privileged position, in the church they often find themselves marginalized, or at least in a minority position.[3] In order for Christians in Myanmar to break out of this isolation and make a significant impact in this largely Buddhist country, the church may need to abandon its strong ethnic identity and embrace a more inclusive ecclesiology.

The purpose of this book is to explore an understanding of the church as an inclusive multiethnic fellowship, modeling a diverse yet united community. This will require a rethinking of the nature of the church grounded in reconciliation between the various ethnic groups within the Myanmar church.[4] Bringing Christians from various ethnicities together may in turn lead to a more

---

1. After many years of hard work in the port city of Yangon, Adoniram Judson could count only a handful of Bamar believers. But not long after new mission stations were opened in Tavoy (Dawei), significant numbers of Karen and other minorities had become Christians. Maung Shwe Wa, *Burma Baptist Chronicle*, ed. Genevieve Sowards and Erville Sowards (Rangoon: Burma Baptist Convention, 1963), 67–70.

2. Thant Myint-U, *The River of Lost Footsteps: A Personal History of Burma* (London: Faber & Faber, 2007), 210–11.

3. Samuel Ngun Ling, *Christianity through Our Neighbors' Eyes: Rethinking the 200 Years Old American Baptist Missions in Myanmar* (Yangon: Judson Research Center, MIT, 2014), 45, 47, 51. "Since Christianity was, to a large extent, accepted by the ethnic minority groups whom the Burmans regard as ethically inferior to them, it was . . . difficult for [the Burmans] to accept such a minority religion."

4. Throughout this study the term "the Myanmar church" will be used to refer to the national church or the churches in Myanmar as a whole.

inclusive community where people from all ethnic and religious backgrounds feel welcome.

Consequently, we will engage in a biblical-theological exploration of essential characteristics of the church in the context of a pluralist society. These characteristics include the church as a community of believers who are called out both from and into the world, and the church as a body united in fellowship. Moreover, the church is a multiethnic mosaic that brings together people from a variety of ethnocultural backgrounds. A number of key New Testament passages will be examined to draw out the implications of reconciliation with God and with one another.

For the church in Myanmar to live out its calling as a missional community, it needs to embrace and demonstrate reconciliation, both within the church and in society in general. Various internal challenges confront the church, such as disunity manifested in ethnic denominationalism that hinders its witness by creating the impression of a fragmented community, reinforcing the perception of the church as a collection of monocultural communities. The clergy-laity division seriously hampers the role of church members by restricting ministry to those who have been officially appointed. Additionally, there is serious need for reflection on contextualization of the Christian message and traditions. More attention also needs to be given to developing a more outward-focused model of discipleship that not only promotes individual spiritual growth, but also seeks to transform the community. These challenges, both separately and together, will require a thorough rethinking of what it means to be a church in a multicultural, multireligious, and multiethnic society.

Chapter 1 will examine how the present condition resulted from a combination of historical, political, and religious factors. The second chapter will consider some missiological, ecclesiological, and theological dynamics that played a role in shaping and molding the church into its present form. Chapter 3 sets out to evaluate relevant theological contributions regarding the essence and mission of the church, particularly the implications for the church in a multicultural context. These findings will be assessed in chapter 4 in light of a biblical-theological study of the nature of the church, its redemptive purpose in the world, and its calling to be a reconciling, unifying, and missional community. Finally, we will suggest a strategy to encourage churches to adopt a spiritual formation focus and embrace ethnic diversity, engaging the whole membership in contextualized ministry.

Part 1

Myanmar in Context

1

Community Context in Myanmar

Throughout its long and sometimes violent history, Myanmar[1] has struggled to attain unity and harmony among its various ethnic populations. Even after gaining independence from British domination, the country has been plagued by ethnic conflict between the majority Bamar and the ethnic minorities.[2] To a lesser extent there has also been ongoing tension and conflict among some of the minorities themselves.

The Postcolonial Legacy

The Republic of the Union of Myanmar (or Burma, as it was formerly known when it was part of the British Empire) is not a homogeneous society. It resembles more a multicolor ethnic mosaic, or as Mikael Gravers characterizes the country, "multi-ethnic, multi-religious and multicultural contexts of the modern nation-state of the Union of Burma."[3] Ever since the country gained independence in 1947, it has struggled to maintain its unity. Until the British conquered Burma after three Anglo-Burmese wars in the nineteenth century, the country had never been a true unitary state. Most areas of the present-day Chin, Kachin, Shan, and Karen States were never firmly under the control of the Burmese throne, while the Rakhine and Mon peoples submitted to Burmese rule only reluctantly and under pressure.[4]

---

1. "Myanmar" will be used when speaking about the country after its name was changed in 1989 and "Burma" when speaking about the country before the change.

2. Thant Myint-U, *River of Lost Footsteps*, 8, 21; Mikael Gravers, ed., *Exploring Ethnic Diversity in Burma*, 1st ed., NIAS Studies in Asian Topics (Copenhagen: Nordic Institute of Asian Studies, 2006), 55.

3. Gravers, *Exploring Ethnic Diversity in Burma*, 201.

4. Thant Myint-U, *River of Lost Footsteps*, 109–10.

The Shan, living in relative isolation on the Shan plateau of Eastern Burma, used to enjoy a certain level of autonomy, depending on the strength of the Burmese rulers in the lowland areas. In exchange, they paid tribute to the Burmese Court.[5] To the south, on the Tenasserim coast, lived the Mon, longtime adversaries and rivals of the Burmans. After the Burmese victory over the Mon by King Alaungpaya and the sacking of their capital Pegu (Bago) in 1755, the Mon were never again able to challenge Burmese hegemony.[6] A similar fate befell the Arakanese of the Western Burma coastal region, after their defeat by the Burmese army in 1784.[7] Like the Mon, the Arakanese (or Rakhine as they are better known nowadays) were never again able to recover their independence, but to this day they remain staunchly proud of their ethnic identity. The Karen, living in the jungles of Eastern Burma and the Irrawaddy River delta, were never a military or political threat to the Burmese and preferred to keep to themselves, although they were often forced to work as serfs to their powerful Burmese rulers.[8] Only with the arrival of the British and the conversion of many to Christianity were the Karen elevated from their subservient status, gaining some measure of respect and self-confidence.[9] The Chin, living in the remote and inaccessible western Chin Hills, were frequently harassed and raided by the lowland Burmese, but their isolation meant they were never fully conquered by them.[10] The Kachin of Northern Burma were probably the most successful of all minorities in defying Burmese control. Their fierce resistance ensured their relative in spite of persistent efforts from both Burmese and Chinese to subjugate them.[11]

With Myanmar being wedged between two superpowers, India and China, the rulers of its various kingdoms and territories have had to carefully position themselves throughout history in order to maintain a certain level of

---

5. Shona T. S. Goodman, *From Princess to Persecuted: A Condensed History of the Shan/Tai to 1962* (n.p.: CreateSpace Independent Publishing Platform, 2014), 81.

6. Gravers, *Exploring Ethnic Diversity in Burma*, 151; John F. Cady, *A History of Modern Burma* (Ithaca, NY: Cornell University Press, 1958), 34.

7. Thant Myint-U, *River of Lost Footsteps*, 109–10; Richard Cockett, *Blood, Dreams and Gold: The Changing Face of Burma* (New Haven: Yale University Press, 2015), 36.

8. Gravers, *Exploring Ethnic Diversity in Burma*, 7, 246; Cockett, *Blood, Dreams and Gold*, 132–33.

9. Thant Myint-U, *River of Lost Footsteps*, 211; Gravers, 242; Milton Osborne, *Southeast Asia: An Introductory History*, 9th ed. (Crows Nest, Australia: Allen & Unwin, 2004), 249.

10. Gravers, 206.

11. Thant Myint-U, *River of Lost Footsteps*, 195; Gravers, 12.

independence.[12] This balance of power was drastically altered with the arrival of Western colonial powers in the region, starting in the sixteenth and seventeenth centuries. The eastward expansion of the British Empire finally resulted in the conquest of and control over all of present-day Myanmar.[13]

To focus on the colonial period of Burma is not to deny the long and fascinating history of this strategic country that forms a bridge between India to the west, China to the north, and Southeast Asia. However, for the purpose of studying the history and present state of the church, the period of colonial rule has been the most influential factor. The reason for this is that, while British rule of Burma lasted less than a century, it left a lasting impact on the country, as it not only provided opportunities for missionary work, but also created an enduring aversion toward Christianity as a colonial religion.

Buddhism and Other Religions

According to Burmese tradition, the introduction of Buddhism dates back to the earliest days of the Buddha, when two traveling Burmese merchants brought back eight of his hairs which were enshrined in what later became known as the Shwedagon Pagoda. This is Myanmar's most revered religious symbol, although the present-day structure is from a much later date, perhaps five centuries old.[14] But it was not until the second century AD that Buddhism began to spread through Southeast Asia, primarily through trade connections across the Bay of Bengal with South India. Within a few hundred years, Buddhism had become the dominant religion in the city-states of the Ayeyarwady (also known as Irrawaddy) River valley. The historian Thant Myint-U calls this "the single most important development in Burma's long history," as it would determine Burma's religious, social, and cultural environment until the present day.[15] When the invading Bamar came down from Nanzhao in Southern China and established their kingdom centered in Bagan along the Ayeyarwady River they adopted the Theravada (Hinayana) strand of Buddhism, constructing the largest collection of Buddhist pagodas in the world.[16] Throughout the rise and

---

12. Thant Myint-U, *Where China Meets India: Burma and the New Crossroads of Asia* (New York: Farrar, Straus and Giroux, 2011), 77–79.

13. Thant Myint-U, *Where China Meets India*, 238; Andrew Marshall, *The Trouser People: Burma in the Shadows of the Empire* (Bangkok: River Books, 2012), 48.

14. Marshall, *Trouser People*, 49.

15. Marshall, 51.

16. Thant Myint-U, *River of Lost Footsteps*, 56–57; Shway Yoe (aka Sir James George Scott), *The Burman: His Life and Notions* (New York: Norton, 1963), 173.

fall of dynasties and kingdoms, Buddhism remained the principal unifying factor for the people of Myanmar. Whether centered around the Mon capital, Bago (Pegu), or later at Ava, near Mandalay, Buddhism provided each ruler and his people with the moral, spiritual, and social frameworks to foster unity and cohesion.[17]

It is evident that Buddhism has deeply influenced and shaped the Burmese worldview. According to missiologist Paul Hiebert, "our worldview is made up of our fundamental assumptions about the nature of reality. It is the way 'things really are' – the picture of the world that we perceive to be true for everyone."[18] Underlying our worldviews are different belief systems that "make explicit the implicit assumptions of the worldview within which they function and apply these assumptions to beliefs and behavior."[19] Consequently, the Buddhist belief in karma permeates the Bamar worldview, to the point that every life experience is seen as a result of past actions or inactions.[20]

Religion in this majority Buddhist country pervades virtually all areas of life. From the monks doing the alms rounds in the morning to the laypeople earning merit by offering them food, from the throngs of worshippers visiting the numerous pagodas on Buddhist holy days to the pious individuals committing to several days of quiet meditation in order to attain peace of mind, daily life for most Burmese revolves around religious practices promising a spiritual benefit.[21] For many Burmese, selling garlands and candles, erecting statues and images of the Buddha, and even engaging in fortune-telling have become a way of life, providing a reasonably adequate income in a country where a significant proportion of the population still lives below the poverty line.

While most people acknowledge the Buddhist idea that one's life is governed by (present and past) karma, they are also convinced that their lives are controlled by fate, luck, and the activity of various spirits (*nats*)

---

17. Edward A. Irons, *Encyclopedia of Buddhism*, Encyclopedia of World Religions (New York: Infobase Publishing, 2006), 350–51.

18. Paul G. Hiebert, *Anthropological Reflections on Missiological Issues* (Grand Rapids, MI: Baker, 1994), 10.

19. Hiebert, *Anthropological Reflections*, 37. See also Charles H. Kraft, *Anthropology for Christian Witness*, 2nd ed. (Maryknoll, NY: Orbis, 1997), 58–63.

20. Melford E. Spiro, *Buddhism and Society: A Great Tradition and Its Burmese Vicissitudes*, 2nd ed. (Berkeley: University of California Press, 1982), 92–93, 99.

21. Spiro, *Buddhism and Society*, 94. Spiro points out that in original (nibbanic) Buddhism the central concept is knowledge. However, in the everyday experience of the average Burmese, Buddhist knowledge as the way to enlightenment and nirvana has been replaced by meritorious acts. For most Buddhists the goal in life is the improvement of one's karma, rather than its extinction.

and other supernatural forces.[22] As such, both Buddhism and animism (or supernaturalism, as some writers describe it) attempt to deal with the problem of suffering by offering an explanation for suffering and providing ways to alleviate or avoid it. Burmese animism manifests itself in a variety of ways, such as ghosts, demons, witches, and what the Burmese call *nats*,[23] who need to be placated or else they may cause harm to human beings. While Buddhism provides an explanation for the origin of suffering, namely karma, the result of one's good and bad deeds done in the past, it does not offer a way of escape from the consequences of this karma. It can only offer a way to prevent future suffering by eliminating the desire that produced the karma and that led to the suffering. Supernaturalism, however, not only gives a different explanation for the cause of suffering, but it also offers a way out of present adversity.[24]

While most Burmese would consider themselves Buddhists first and foremost, their actual religious practices reveal that dealing with the supernatural is at least as relevant to them. Thus, they often engage in ceremonies designed to appease these spiritual forces. In fact, sometimes offerings and prayers can be made to *nats* and Buddha images at the same festival or pilgrimage. Since the *nat* cultus preceded the introduction of Buddhism in Burma, we may assume that many sacred places were originally *nat* shrines, and only later became places of Buddhist worship.[25] This process provided Buddhist legitimacy to the *nats* and helped to show the primacy of Buddhism.[26] Even though many Western commentators consider Buddhism primarily a philosophical (i.e. non-supernatural) belief system, canonical Buddhism explicitly affirms the

---

22. See among others, Maung Htin Aung, *Folk Elements in Burmese Buddhism* (Yangon: Religious Affairs Department, 1959); Melford E. Spiro, *Burmese Supernaturalism* (Englewood Cliffs, NJ: Prentice-Hall, 1967). Spiro argues that Buddhism and supernaturalism exist side by side in the Burmese worldview. He explains that most people have compartmentalized their religion and do not see any conflict between different spheres of life. Cf. also Spiro, *Buddhism and Society*, 186–87.

23. According to Spiro, witches are humans, while *nats* are spirits. Ghosts, while similar to *nats*, are terrestrial, whereas *nats* appear in a nonhuman form. The latter are part of an elaborate system of thirty-seven *nats* who are widely revered (and feared) in Myanmar. One common characteristic of these *nats* is that they died a violent death, and are therefore considered malevolent. Spiro, *Buddhism and Society*, 41.

24. Interestingly, since animism blames evil witches, harmful *nats*, or ghosts for one's suffering, it removes personal responsibility from the individual. He or she is merely the victim, having wittingly or unwittingly offended the spirit. In any case, people are able to remedy their predicament by making restitution through an offering or other ritual. Cf. Spiro, 4.

25. Maung Maung Aye, "Spirit Belief in Burmese Buddhism: A Buddhist Perspective," *Engagement*, Judson Research Center Bulletin (Myanmar Institute of Theology) 7 (Dec. 2006): 49.

26. "Pagodas are always erected near a *nat* shrine so that people should not forget the Buddha even if they come to propitiate the *nats*." Spiro, *Burmese Supernaturalism*, 250.

existence of a variety of spirits, both good and evil. It even teaches that these spirits may be coerced and exorcised by the recitation of certain sutras:

> Contrary . . . to some Buddhist intellectuals and to most Western critics of Burmese *nats*, animistic beliefs as well as rituals are perfectly compatible with orthodox Buddhism, even with the Buddhism of the Pali Canon. Their alleged incompatibility stems from the false assumption that "pure" Buddhism is – or, at least in its original form, was – an exclusively ethical system, devoid of supernatural beliefs and rites.[27]

The recitation of *pareittas* to ward off evil continues to be an important function of Buddhist monks. In addition, some monks are famous as exorcists (*athelan hsaya*). The Buddhist rosary is often used as a talisman, and praying through one's beads is deemed especially effective in warding off evil spirits. The yellow robe of the monk is considered extremely powerful, and the most effective way of escaping from attack by evil forces is to become a monk.

Nevertheless, there are serious incompatibilities between *nat* belief and practice on the one hand, and the Buddhist doctrine of karma on the other. The first conflict is doctrinal. Given the principle of karma, the propitiation of the *nats* is futile; they cannot harm a person whose karma is good, and conversely, if one's karma is bad, one will suffer harm in some manner anyway. If, on the other hand, harmful spirits caused the suffering, one can contest rather than accept it, by placating the spirits. In short, the belief in *nats* allows the Burmese to avoid the painful consequences of a consistent belief in karma. When religious norms are inconsistent with personal needs, the latter will usually prevail, according to Spiro:

> In theory, those acts which increase one's store of merit yield their karmic consequences in one's next existence. However, when faced with trouble, the Burmese perform meritorious acts with the hope not merely of affecting their future karma, but also of altering their present karma. Although the latter, having been determined by one's past actions, is unalterable in principle, the Burmese venerate relics, worship the Buddha, say their beads, offer food to monks, and so on, with the expectation that the good karma which is thereby accumulated will nullify the bad karma which is responsible for their present ills.[28]

---

27. Spiro, 251.
28. Spiro, 256.

The second conflict between Buddhism and animism is ethical. The two systems are diametrically opposed in various dimensions, as table 1 by Melford Spiro indicates.[29]

Table 1. Differences between Buddhism and *Nat* Cultus

Dimension	Buddhism	*Nat* Cultus
Morality	moral	amoral
Sensuality	ascetic	libertarian
Reason	rational	nonrational
Personality	serene	turbulent
Society	otherworldly	worldly

Buddhism is, at its core, a moral system. Moral behavior, in fact, is the only way to acquire merit, which determines one's karma and therefore one's future. *Nats*, on the other hand, are indifferent to morality, so that "the criminal who propitiates a *nat* will be the object of his favors, and the saint who neglects him will be the victim of his punishment."[30] Buddhism holds that only by eliminating desire will one attain nirvana, whereas the *nat* cultus is often an occasion for sensual gratification, even license. Furthermore, the Buddha arrived at his conviction by observation and logical reasoning: if desire causes suffering, then eradicating desire can eliminate suffering. Meditating on this truth leads to nirvana. In contrast, placation of the *nats* is motivated by fear, and spiritual truths are discovered by possession. Next, while the Buddhist ideal is characterized by serenity, the shamans are characterized by their frenzied dancing, wild gestures, shouting, and screaming. Finally, Buddhism's orientation is fundamentally otherworldly, since the visible world is temporary, illusionary, and marked by suffering. Salvation for the Buddhist is escape from this present existence. Animism on the other hand seeks to escape suffering by controlling the circumstances affecting our existence in this world.

It is therefore evident that Buddhism and animism are distinct, even contrasting, systems, each operating in its own sphere of life. The *nat* cultus focuses on the here and now, whereas Buddhism is primarily concerned with future outcomes, although its followers sometimes seek to achieve temporary goals as well. In all this, Buddhism is considered far superior to the animistic

---

29. Adapted from: "A Comparison of Some Salient Dimensions of Buddhism and the *Nat* Cultus, Viewed as Ideal Types," Spiro, 258.

30. Spiro, 259.

practices governing much of Burmese daily life. While animist values tend to be consistent with Burmese needs and drives, Buddhist values are more in line with their aspired values.[31] This prompts the question as to why the two systems continue to operate side by side, instead of one being taken over by the other. It would seem that animism provides a non-Buddhist solution for those needs that are ignored or prohibited by Buddhism, and thus allows Buddhism to remain insulated from imperfection. It allows the Burmese to seek remedies for their immediate needs through animistic means, while at the same time worshipping the Buddha and the monks as idealized objects of veneration.

These observations have implications for Christian ministry and for approaches to gospel communication in particular. In order to respond to felt needs of Myanmar Buddhists, it will be necessary to focus not only on their Buddhist beliefs and worldview, but also on their deeply held animist (supernaturalist) beliefs and practices. Cross-cultural proclamation of the good news will need to carefully consider how to appropriately address both realities.

Bamar Pride and Prejudice

The history of Burma has long been characterized by the struggle of the Burmans to control the non-Burman segments of the population, and by non-Burman resistance to these efforts.[32] During certain periods in history the Burmans succeeded in establishing a measure of control over the Shan, Kachin, Karen, and other minority groups that make up Burma's ethnic mosaic, while at other times these minorities were able to reassert a measure of autonomy.[33] Under British colonial rule the Burmans lost some of their dominant role, as the colonial powers favored other ethnic groups with preferential treatment. However, after independence, the old interethnic tensions reemerged. These continue to pose one of the most significant problems for the country, even after more than sixty years of independence.[34] While Burma has sought to

---

31. "For most Burmese, animism is a concession to human frailty; Buddhism is a striving for human nobility. Animism represents man's natural fears and desires, Buddhism symbolizes his highest ideals and aspirations. Animism presents man as he is; Buddhism indicates what he ought to be (and can become)." Spiro, 273.

32. The term "Burman" is used here to distinguish those of Burman ethnicity from other Burmese ethnic groups, whereas the term "Burmese" is mostly used to refer to the population of Burma in general or, at least, when no distinction between various ethnicities is made. Sometimes the term "Bamar" is used instead of "Burman," both terms being considered synonymous here.

33. Osborne, *Southeast Asia*, 65.

34. Osborne, 228.

carve its own way into the future through the Burmese Way to Socialism,[35] the fact is that ethnic rivalry remains an important component in Burmese history, both classic and modern.[36]

For hundreds of years, Buddhism has been at the heart of Burmese society. The monkhood touches virtually every segment of society and holds the people's reverence. Pagoda shrines built to acquire merit dot the countryside in all areas and each village has at least one monastery. The number of monks and neophytes is commonly estimated at between 300,000 and 500,000, or about one in thirty of all adult males. It might be said that Buddhism, in particular the monkhood (*Sangha*), held together the religious, cultural, and even political civilization of ancient Burma. It was the bond that connected the Bamar with the Rakhine, Mon, and Shan populations. It is no wonder, therefore, that the arrival of Christian missionaries seeking to end these traditions was seen as a threat to national identity and unity.

Historically, Burmese youth around the age of eight were sent to the monastery for schooling. These young *kyaungtha* waited on the older *upasin* and *pongyi* at meals, accompanied them on their morning alms-receiving rounds, drew water as needed, and cared for the monastic quarters in general. They also learned to read and write, and memorized Buddhist commandments and Pali formulas used in pagoda rituals.[37] These traditions endure to the present day, and continue to influence and mold young Buddhist men. The minimum period for ordination of a novice is one Lenten season, about three months. Although most young people sooner or later return to life as laypeople, many stay on into adulthood and some spend the rest of their lives in the monastery.[38]

Buddhism in Burma, however, has also had strong political and nationalist overtones. The famous monk Saya San had ambitions to become the next Burmese king and led the rebellion against the British in 1930, and it took the colonial army two years to subdue him and his followers. Widespread student-led demonstrations in 1938 and 1939 were joined by thousands of Buddhist monks, highlighting the monks' political and social involvement.[39]

---

35. The Burmese Way to Socialism refers to the ideology of the socialist government in Burma after the 1962 coup d'état led by General Ne Win. It served as a blueprint to reduce foreign influence in Burma and increase the role of the military.

36. Osborne, *Southeast Asia*, 278–79.

37. Shway Yoe, *The Burman*, 30–38.

38. Cady, *History of Modern Burma*, 58.

39. Thant Myint-U, *River of Lost Footsteps*, 216.

Students protesting military rule in 1988 were widely supported by Buddhist monks.[40] In 2007 the monks featured prominently in the Saffron Revolution, the name referring to the color of the monks' robes. While these efforts have been widely praised as honorable initiatives, Buddhism in Myanmar also has a darker side, fueled by regularly resurfacing racist nationalism. The Buddhist monk-led anti-Muslim demonstrations in 2012 are an example of this extreme nationalism, used by the authorities to promote national identity. While the 2007 Saffron Revolution sought to restore democracy to Myanmar, the 2012 protests were aimed at removing the most despised (and unrecognized) minority, the Rohingya, from the country.[41]

While government authorities occasionally acknowledge the country's ethnic diversity, in general the Buddhist Bamar are considered the backbone of national identity.[42] Aung Thu Nyein of the Vahu Development Institute says that the Bamar majority has consistently prevented non-Buddhist minorities from occupying positions of authority, asserting that "they don't have any written laws and regulations, but practically, in the military if you are a Christian or if you are a Muslim you won't be promoted up to major ranks. You won't be a senior leader in the military."[43] This statement underscores the delicate position of those serving in the army who belong to minority religions. There have also been multiple reports of government attempts to convert Christian and other minorities to Buddhism.[44] One method is to force children to attend state-sponsored schools where they receive Buddhist instruction, often with

---

40. Michael W. Charney, *A History of Modern Burma* (Cambridge: Cambridge University Press, 2008), 153–54.

41. Daniel Schearf, "Authorities Nurture Burma's Buddhist Chauvinism, Analysts Say," VOA News, 7 September 2012, accessed 19 July 2017, https://www.voanews.com/a/burma_buddhist_chauvinism_nurtured_by_authorities/1503665.html. Further violence erupted in October 2016 and again in August 2017. Responding to an attack by the Arakan Rohingya Salvation Army (ARSA), the Burmese army carried out widespread "clearance operations" forcing over 700,000 Rohingya to flee to Bangladesh in the span of a few months.

42. "Burmans are generally privileged politically, economically and socially vis-à-vis non-Burmans." Matthew J. Walton, "The 'Wages of Burman-ness': Ethnicity and Burman Privilege in Contemporary Myanmar," *Journal of Contemporary Asia* 43, no. 1 (2013): 6, accessed 24 July 2019, https://www.tandfonline.com/doi/full/10.1080/00472336.2012.730892.

43. Schearf, "Authorities Nurture Burma's Buddhist Chauvinism." See also Walton, "Wages of Burman-Ness," 24; Khin Mai Aung, "Why Myanmar Must Develop an Identity of Inclusion," Lion's Roar, 28 February 2019, accessed 23 July 2019, https://www.lionsroar.com/commentary-why-myanmar-must-develop-an-identity-of-inclusion/; International Commission of Jurists, *Challenges to Freedom of Religion or Belief in Myanmar: A Briefing Paper* (Geneva: International Commission of Jurists, October 2019), 8.

44. Charlie Campbell, "Christian Chin 'Coerced to Buddhism by State,'" The Irrawaddy, 5 September 2012, accessed 12 September 2017, http://www.irrawaddy.org/burma/christian-chin-coerced-to-buddhism-by-state.html.

the assistance of Buddhist monks. One such report, by the Chin Human Rights Organization (CHRO), based on over one hundred interviews, details the following:

> There are 29 Na Ta La (Border Areas National Races Youth Development Training) schools across Burma, primarily targeting ethnic and religious minorities. The schools function outside the mainstream, chronically underfunded education system and practice targeted recruitment of impoverished Chin who lack the means to pay for alternative schooling. Ethnic Chin make up one-third of students at Na Ta La schools where they are prevented from practicing Christianity and instead coerced to convert to Buddhism, primarily via the threat of military conscription. Students are often forced to shave their heads and wear robes of monks or nuns.[45]

Even in more urban areas with a mixed population, non-Buddhist students are often forced to participate in Buddhist ceremonies and rituals, and classes or exams are often scheduled on Sundays, particularly during Buddhist Lent.[46] All in all, it may be said that Buddhism makes full use of its dominant position in society to extend its influence. It may not formally be the state religion intended by U Nu, prime minister of Burma during several periods from independence in 1948 until the military takeover in 1962, but it operates as such.[47]

Further, the 969 Movement[48] takes its name from the Buddhist tradition of the Three Jewels or Trairatana, which are composed of twenty-four attributes (nine for the Buddha, six for the Dhamma, nine for the Sangha). It seeks to

45. Unrepresented Nations and Peoples Organization, "Chin: New Report Sheds Light on Religious Discrimination," 10 September 2012, accessed 6 November 2017, http://www.unpo.org/article/14830.

46. This is an oft aired complaint within the Christian community. Some of these issues are merely a consequence of Buddhist traditions, such as the custom to move classes to the weekend when a festival day falls on a weekday during Lent. However, such practices do create friction and resentment when they affect the ability to attend church on a Sunday.

47. "Buddhism and State Power in Myanmar," International Crisis Group, Report 290, 5 September 2017, accessed 11 April 2022, https://www.crisisgroup.org/asia/south-east-asia/myanmar/290-buddhism-and-state-power-myanmar. Also Kosak Tuscangate, "Burmese Neo-Nazi Movement Rising against Muslims," The Irrawaddy, 24 March 2013, accessed 6 November 2017, https://www.irrawaddy.com/opinion/guest-column/burmese-neo-nazi-movement-rising-against-muslims.html.

48. The 969 Movement is a nationalist movement opposed to what its adherents see as Islam's expansion in predominantly Buddhist Burma.

promote Buddhism as the dominant force in society and to combat the threat posed by Islam by, for example, boycotting Muslim shops and businesses.[49] In another development, a few years ago Buddhist nationalist monks established the Organization for the Protection of Race and Religion (*Amyo Batha Thathana Kakwe Saungshaukyay Apwe* or *Ma-Ba-Tha*). Under pressure from this Buddhist monk-led movement, Parliament in 2015 adopted four religion and marriage laws that restrict religious conversion and interfaith marriage and polygamy, and promote family planning.[50]

Problematic Interethnic Relations

The British discovered that, in order to rule Burma, they needed to use direct rule only in the Bamar areas, that is, the central plains. The minority areas where the Chin, Kachin, Shan, Karen, and Kayah lived were allowed greater autonomy, as their loyalty was much less in dispute.[51] This division would end up creating many complications when Burma became independent, due to ill feeling between the different ethnic groups. Ethnic tensions also arose as the British brought an increasing number of Indians into the country, many of whom took government jobs. Some of them became relatively wealthy by starting their own businesses. The less business-savvy Burmese were unable to compete with them.[52] Resentment against these groups on the part of the Burmese persists to the present day.

After independence, fighting broke out on multiple fronts between ethnic rebel groups, communists, gangs, and anti-communist Chinese KMT forces supported by the United States. The hill tribe people, who had supported the British and fought against the Japanese during the Second World War, did not trust the Bamar majority and took up arms.[53] The communists withdrew from the government and instead opted to fight for their cause. Muslims from Rakhine State also turned against the new government, and even the Mon,

---

49. Matthew J. Walton and Susan Hayward, *Contesting Buddhist Narratives: Democratization, Nationalism, and Communal Violence in Myanmar*, Policy Studies 71 (Honolulu: East-West Center, 2014), 14.

50. Nyi Nyi Kyaw, "Myanmar's Rising Buddhist Nationalism: Impact on Foreign Investors," RSIS Commentaries, 2, 15 May 2014, accessed 6 November 2017, http://www.rsis.edu.sg/wp-content/uploads/2014/09/CO14090.pdf; International Commission of Jurists, *Challenges to Freedom of Religion*, 23–24.

51. Thant Myint-U, *River of Lost Footsteps*, 211; Osborne, *Southeast Asia*, 204.

52. Charney, *History of Modern Burma*, 37–40.

53. Walton, "Wages of Burman-Ness," 9.

long thought to have assimilated with the Burmese, turned against them. It took almost two years for the Burmese army to regain control over most of the country, although many of the border areas remained under the control of various ethnic armies.

When the State Law and Order Restoration Council (SLORC) took power in 1988, it introduced a new framework of 135 national races of Myanmar. This new categorization was introduced "as a direct critique and dismissal of the eight 'big races' – the Burmans, the Mon, the Shan, the Karen, the Kayah (Karenni), the Kachin, the Chin, and the Rakhine (Arakanese) – the major categories used during the colonial rule."[54] The choice of 135 groups may have originated with the languages listed in the 1931 British census. However, the decision by the SLORC to count all the different groups in each state and add them together resulted in counting some groups more than once if they were listed in more than one state. Moreover, the Bamar were counted wherever they lived, while Kayin were included only in Kayin State, even though there are many Kayin living in Ayeyarwady, Bago, and Yangon divisions.[55]

The continuing struggle between the Bamar-dominated army and the various ethnic minorities is a clear demonstration of an ideological and existential battle to impose their own vision of the world, and to confirm their identity and cultural legacy. Mikael Gravers even goes so far as to say that "the conflict in Burma is not an inter-ethnic conflict but a protracted post-colonial conflict between the state represented by the military with its vision of a unitary nation state and ethnic groups struggling to obtain territorial and cultural autonomy as legitimate national entities."[56] Matthew Walton, writing in the *Journal of Contemporary Asia*, argues that Bamar people have enjoyed a privileged position in Myanmar society, akin to white privilege, even though many of them have also experienced a level of suffering at the hands of the military. However, "this shared sense of suffering itself blinds most Burmans to their own privileged position and to the discrimination and atrocities that non-Burmans disproportionately experience."[57] The Bamar therefore tend to downplay the suffering of the minorities, seeing themselves as equally victimized by the atrocities of the regime.

The social, religious, and historical dynamics described in this chapter – the damaging legacy of colonialism, the pervasive influence of Buddhism, the

---

54. Gravers, *Exploring Ethnic Diversity in Burma*, 4.
55. Gravers, 4. Also, Walton, "Wages of Burman-Ness," 6.
56. Gravers, 8.
57. Walton, "Wages of Burman-Ness," 20.

dominant position of the Bamar, and the lasting impact of ethnic rivalries – together have created formidable barriers for the reception of the gospel among the people of Myanmar. Each of them separately poses an enormous barrier for establishing a truly indigenous church in this country. Together they reveal the daunting task awaiting the church in its calling to be missional in this context. This undertaking is further complicated by the internal challenges confronting the church in Myanmar, which will be explored in the next chapter.

2

Ministry Context in Myanmar

While Buddhism has dominated Myanmar for more than fifteen centuries, Christianity appeared only some three hundred years ago with the arrival of Portuguese and other traders.[1] With Christianity mostly confined to the foreign community, very few locals adopted the religion of these outsiders.[2] Roman Catholic missionaries tried to establish themselves in Burma and expand the Christian community during the seventeenth and eighteenth centuries. Finding themselves caught between opposing groups and factions, the missionaries often became the victims of these groups' anger. Those turbulent years were marked by continual struggles between the Mon in Pegu (Bago) and the Burmese kingdom in Ava (near Mandalay). Foreigners were often suspected of spying for the enemy, leading to the deaths of the missionaries and their followers, either through mob violence or formal execution.[3]

---

1. C. Duh Kam, "Christian Mission to Buddhists in Myanmar: A Study of Past, Present, and Future Approaches by Baptists" (DMiss diss., United Theological Seminary, 1997), 50.

2. Wherever the Portuguese soldiers and merchants went, the priests followed their flock. Portuguese chaplains ministered to them by officiating at marriages and conducting baptisms for their children. The rich kingdom of Pegu began to attract the Portuguese from Malaya, who soon set up more trading stations in Mergui, Tavoy, Syriam, and Bassein. The few Burmese who did embrace Christianity faced severe isolation and prejudice from their fellow citizens, as is evident from this comment: "The few natives that became converts . . . were called Kalar, because in the opinion of the Burmese, they had embraced the religion of the Kalar and had become bona fide strangers, having lost their own nationality." Paul A. Bigandet, *An Outline of the History of the Catholic Mission from 1720 to 1887*, quoted in Kanbawza Win, "The Beginning of the Christian Mission in Burma: 1519–1813," in Christianity in Myanmar Conference, ed. Kawlthangvuta and Johnny Maung Latt (presented at the Christianity in Myanmar Conference, unpublished conference papers. Bethany Theological Seminary, Yangon, Myanmar, 2002), 3.

3. Thant Myint-U, *Where China Meets India*, 79–80, 97; Kam, "Christian Mission to Buddhists in Myanmar," 53.

Once Burma became united under King Alaungpaya the Catholic missionaries had greater freedom to move around and even to open schools across the country. By 1778 there were allegedly over three thousand Christians in Rangoon.[4] Under Alaungpaya's reign (1752–1760) and that of his descendant Bodawpaya (1782–1819) the country attained a measure of unity and was able to minimize external threats from its neighbors.[5] While Burma managed to remedy some of its internal divisions, it soon confronted another, external threat: the British Empire was slowly extending its rule into northeastern India, which the Burmese had until then considered as part of their sphere of influence.

Christianity Seen as a Western Import

Although the first Protestant missionaries (particularly Adoniram and Ann Judson) had arrived in Burma in 1813, before the military engagements with the British army, their progress and setbacks were to a large extent connected with the advance of the colonial powers. In the end, "Burma was carved up by the British over three Anglo-Burmese wars (1824–1826, 1852–1853 and 1885) and for much of the nineteenth century there were two competing Burmas, a shrinking independent state in the north and an expanding colonial entity in the south."[6] Once colonial rule had been established throughout the whole country, British rule began to dominate daily life. The large-scale development of rice cultivation in the Ayeyarwady delta of Lower Myanmar led to increased prosperity and the migration of a large number of Karen and other minorities to this previously sparsely populated area. While the staunchly nationalistic Burmans strongly resented the foreign domination of their country, some of the minorities were much less antagonistic, possibly due to the better conditions they experienced under the British, who tended to get along better with the Karen, entrusting them with responsibilities they had never been given before.[7] According to the historian Thant Myint-U,

> many Karens came to associate British rule and their cooperation
> with the British with a better life and future. In the months after

---

4. Kanbawza Win, "Beginning of the Christian Mission in Burma," 13–14; Kawl Thang Vuta, "A Brief History of the Planting and Growth of the Church in Burma" (DMiss diss., Fuller Theological Seminary, 1983), 39.

5. Osborne, *Southeast Asia*, 73.

6. Charney, *History of Modern Burma*, 4.

7. Thant Myint-U, *River of Lost Footsteps*, 166; Cockett, *Blood, Dreams and Gold*, 132.

[King] Thibaw's downfall, a special levy of Karen soldiers helped patrol the newly won territories, and it was Christian Karens who helped crush a sympathetic uprising in Lower Burma. From then on large numbers of Karens were recruited into the army and military police.[8]

Their relative openness to the gospel resulted in numerous conversions and the establishment of a multitude of churches both in the delta region and in the hill country.

One unintended consequence of the conversion of ethnic minorities and their close interaction with the foreign missionaries was the perception among the Burmans that the Christians had somehow sold their Burmese heritage to the foreigners.[9] When asked to explain, Burmans commonly declare that

Christianity has been considered a weapon for Westerners to take over the country by using the "3-M" method: Missionary, Merchant and the Military. In the beginning the Westerners came to Myanmar for the purpose of Christian Mission. However, when they saw the people were poor, simple, and trusting, the Westerners took advantage of the people. Finally, it led to exploitation, and they became the Merchants. After becoming rich, they set up the Military in order to occupy the land. With this mindset, not only do the Buddhists hesitate to welcome Christianity, but they are suspicious of Christianity as Neo-colonialism.[10]

It is therefore no exaggeration to assert that colonization has been a mixed blessing for the church. While it opened the door for missionaries to enter the country and proclaim the gospel, it also attached a foreign stigma to Christianity that continues to the present day.

---

8. Thant Myint-U, 211.

9. A common saying, frequently heard when talking with Burmese (Buddhist) people, is that "one more Christian means one less Burmese." This has become a major obstacle to the spread of Christianity among the Bamar population, who are almost exclusively Buddhist.

10. Peter Thein Nyunt, interview with the author on Christian witness in Buddhist Myanmar, 18 December 2014.

The Church as a Religious Minority in Myanmar

Despite over two hundred years of Protestant mission work in Myanmar, only a small minority of the Myanmar population consider themselves Christians.[11] Moreover, the vast majority of Christians belong to the country's ethnic minorities, predominantly the Karen, Kachin, and Chin. In effect, Christians in Myanmar have a minority status in a double sense: first, they constitute a small religious community, and second, they form a religious community consisting almost entirely of ethnic minority people. Bamar Buddhist ideology is closely linked with national identity and nationalist rhetoric. Therefore, the fact that Christians belong to a religious minority places them in a vulnerable position. They often experience serious disadvantages in social, educational, and professional areas.[12] Although Christians have generally not experienced the kind of discrimination and prejudice that has come upon the Muslim community, they are nevertheless often restricted in the religious activities they are allowed to carry out.[13] When applying for permission to build or expand a church, they often encounter significant obstacles. In rural areas churches regularly face opposition and harassment from Buddhist monks who seek to curb or restrict Christian activities in their area.[14] Besides a general and

---

11. According to the 2014 population census, carried out with support from the United Nations, Christians make up 6.3 percent of the population, totaling 3,172,479 people. The Republic of the Union of Myanmar, *The 2014 Myanmar Population and Housing Census – The Union Report: Religion Census Report Volume 2-C* (Myanmar: Department of Population, Ministry of Labour, Immigration and Population, July 2016), 3, accessed 7 November 2017, https://myanmar.unfpa.org/sites/default/files/pub-pdf/UNION_2C_Religion_EN.pdf. It should be noted that the actual number of Christians may be higher, given the negative status attached to belonging to a minority religion and the difficulty some people experience when requesting to change their religion on their ID cards.

12. Cf. Zam Khat Kham, "Burmese Nationalism and Christianity in Myanmar: Christian Identity and Witness in Myanmar Today" (PhD diss., Concordia Seminary, 2015), 108, accessed 7 November 2017, http://scholar.csl.edu/phd/22; Hazel Torres, "Christians Being Pushed out of Their Own Church by Buddhist Monks in Myanmar," *Christianity Today*, last modified 8 May 2016, accessed 7 November 2017, https://www.christiantoday.com/article/christians.being. pushed.out.of.their.own.church.by.buddhist.monks.in.myanmar/85599.htm.

13. Compared with the sometimes indiscriminate use of violence against Muslims (especially in Rakhine State, where many identify themselves as Rohingya). However, the Myanmar government does not include this group among the 135 recognized ethnic nationalities and refers to them instead as "Bengalis."

14. For a detailed report on religious persecution of Christian minorities in Myanmar, see Rachel Fleming, *Hidden Plight: Christian Minorities in Myanmar* (United States Commission on International Religious Freedom, December 2016), 9–20, accessed 4 October 2017, https://www.uscirf.gov/sites/default/files/Hidden%20Plight.%20Christian%20Minorities%20in%20Burma.pdf. The report lists numerous practices that constitute violations of religious freedom, such as "violations of the right to choose own beliefs," "institutionalized discrimination on the basis of religion," "discriminatory restrictions on land ownership for religious purposes,"

widespread dislike of Christianity as a foreign religion, this perspective also reveals a disdain of Christians as members of "ethnic minority groups whom the Burmans regard as morally inferior to them."[15]

Naturally, such attitudes have not contributed to the acceptance and integration of Christians in Myanmar society. Consequently, the church faces an uphill battle in its calling to manifest God's love and proclaim his kingdom in Myanmar. In this respect, the colonial legacy has not helped the church to win a hearing among the Bamar, as Ngun Ling observes when he says that "the majorities (Buddhists) tend to look at the minorities, especially Christians (also Muslims in some instances), with political suspicions as part of continuing neo-colonial power that would interfere in the country in many ways."[16] This prevalent suspicion and negative view of the Christian minority forms a significant obstacle in the mission of the church to communicate its message to the Buddhist community in Myanmar.

These outside challenges are further compounded by internal hurdles, such as the attitude of Christians toward Buddhists and adherents of other religions. It is not uncommon to hear Christians expressing strong, negative feelings toward Buddhists in particular, which is not surprising given the prejudice and treatment they have faced in this Bamar-dominated society. Many Christians have suffered deeply for their faith at the hands of Burmese Buddhists.[17] Their intense pain simply surpasses the desire to reach out with the gospel message of reconciliation:

> There is a long history of mistrust. I think, as a Christian, before we share even the gospel with them, maybe it will be good for us to think, do we really love these people, do we really want them to come to know the Lord? In spite of all the mistrust and misunderstanding? Because the Myanmar people probably look down on these minority groups – the way we live, the way we are, and other things . . . For Kachin or Chin or Karen people, once

---

"violations of freedom of religious assembly," "forced relocation and destruction of Christian cemeteries," "occupation, desecration, and destruction of churches and crosses," "imposition of Buddhist infrastructure via state budget mechanisms," and "coerced conversion to Buddhism."

15. Ngun Ling, *Christianity through Our Neighbours' Eyes*, 51. "No matter how widely Christianity is considered a universal religion, it is, to the Burmans, whose great civilization owes its inception to Theravada Buddhism, inferior to Buddhism" (48).

16. Samuel Ngun Ling, "Ethnicity, Religion and Theology in Asia: An Exploration from Myanmar Context," *Engagement*, Judson Research Center Bulletin (MIT) 7 (Dec. 2006): 6.

17. Zam Khat Kham, "Burmese Nationalism and Christianity in Myanmar," 96–97. Many examples can be found in Fleming, *Hidden Plight*, 9–20. Also Gravers, *Exploring Ethnic Diversity in Burma*, 10.

you become their friends, you are a friend forever. So these are
the things that we, the minorities, think about Myanmar people.[18]

Denominational Division an Obstacle for Witness

Even a perfunctory survey of the Christian community in Myanmar will quickly
reveal the high number of Christian organizations and institutions, often
separated along ethnic and linguistic lines. The *Yangon Directory for Church
and Christian Ministries* lists over one hundred Bible schools, seminaries, and
training centers in Yangon alone, as well as over seventy orphanages, and this
list is probably not exhaustive.[19] Most denominations, including the Myanmar
Baptist Convention (MBC), are divided along ethnic lines into Chin, Kachin,
Karen, and other groups (such as Akha, Lisu, Lahu, Mon, Tamil, Shan, and Wa).

One factor behind the proliferation of different institutions is the vast
number of languages and dialects in use throughout Myanmar. However, while
people naturally gather with others who share their language and customs,
many ethnic churches in Yangon use Burmese language in their worship,
so clearly there are factors beyond language involved in these divisions.
The overwhelming number of small independent entities may be due to the
proliferation of foreign-funded initiatives. As Christians worldwide became
aware of the needs in Myanmar, they stepped in to support local initiatives.
Through local pastors and other Christian workers who had studied abroad,
they began to finance small-scale initiatives, such as orphanages that often
cared, not for children without parents, but for children from rural families
whose parents were hoping for better educational options in the city. These
orphanages frequently form the nucleus of newly emerging churches. These,
in turn, have led to the founding of training centers, which evolved into Bible
schools, usually funded by the same individuals and groups who were providing
support to these enterprising pastors. Without foreign funding, many of these
small entities would not have emerged, let alone survived. It is unfortunate
that the genuine concern from the international Christian community has
helped to foster such individualism and fragmentation. This has led to the
establishment of many independent or semi-independent churches, sometimes

---

18. GCZ, interview with the author on Christian witness in Buddhist Myanmar, 12
November 2014.

19. Salay Hta Oke, *Yangon Directory for Church and Christian Ministries* (Yangon: Christian
Media Center, 2006).

loosely aligned with a denomination, but without much accountability, as the finances continue to come from foreign partners.[20]

Another problem is the complication that arises when the original pioneer of these individual ministries dies or is no longer able to continue. When this happens, it raises questions as to who will carry on the ministry, and who will own and control the property as well as other assets. One could ask critical questions, such as: "What is the purpose of these orphanages?" "Is the objective really to help children without parents, or has it become a ministry tool, a quick way to jump-start a new church, and an easy way to raise funds?" "Are the leaders supporting the children, or are the children supporting the leaders?"

Theological Education in the Myanmar Context

Not long after the establishment of the first Protestant churches in Myanmar, Christian education became a focal point of mission work by the various mission societies in the country. One of the earliest educational institutions, St. John's School, was founded in 1863 by the Anglican mission (nowadays known as The Church of the Province of Myanmar) under J. E. Marks, while Holy Cross Theological Seminary was initiated to provide theological education and pastoral training.[21] The Myanmar Methodist Church (divided into Upper and Lower Myanmar) founded the Myanmar Theological College in Mandalay for the training of its ministers.[22]

The Myanmar Institute of Theology (MIT; previously known as Burma Institute of Theology, and originally named Willis and Orlinda Pierce Divinity College) was established in 1927. It is the largest theological institution in Myanmar, offering several graduate programs (MTh, MACS, MDiv and MTL), as well as doctoral programs (PhD and DMin). It is governed by the Myanmar Baptist Convention, and is accredited with the Association of Theological

---

20. In Myanmar foreigners cannot buy property in their own name. It has to be bought by a local person and that local person does not hand control to the organization or denomination. Since the documents are in the individual's name, the denomination has very little control or authority. "It's one of the things here that I find quite a dangerous situation. . . . I'm not saying we should not help, but . . . donors should find a way to make them accountable to the things that we give them as well. Unfortunately, some people want to be accountable to their leadership but their leadership makes it difficult for them too. For example, someone might want to help this guy in a ministry, but they want the money to come through the organization. Then the organization makes it difficult [complicated] for them. So sometimes they want to donate directly." GCZ , interview with the author.

21. Samuel Ngun Ling, *Communicating Christ in Myanmar: Issues, Interactions and Perspectives*, 3rd ed. (Yangon: Judson Research Center, MIT, 2014), 113.

22. Ngun Ling, *Communicating Christ in Myanmar*, 114.

Education in Southeast Asia (ATESEA). While education at MIT is offered in English, MICT (Myanmar Institute of Christian Theology) and KBTS (Karen Baptist Theological Seminary) use Burmese as their medium of education.[23] The Myanmar Evangelical Graduate School of Theology (MEGST), founded in 1996 by the Myanmar Evangelical Christian Fellowship (now called Myanmar Evangelical Christian Alliance), is the foremost evangelical theological institution, and is accredited by the ATA (Asia Theological Association). In addition to these, there are, as noted above, well over one hundred theological colleges and seminaries throughout Myanmar, many of which are located in and around Yangon.[24]

Several people have commented that this proliferation of Bible schools and training centers has had unfortunate consequences.[25] The first challenge has been a fragmentation of educational resources. The large number of training institutes has led to severe fragmentation in terms of finance, teaching staff, and library resources. Since most students are not able to pay the already modest fees, there is significant competition for sponsorships from abroad. As with the establishment of Christian orphanages,[26] the need for outside funding has spawned competition in the search for donors.[27] Most Bible schools count only a small number of students (often no more than twenty to thirty) and no more than a few faculty members. Many small-church pastors supplement their meager income by teaching part-time at one or several of these small schools. The second challenge is the low standard of education offered at these small establishments. The few teachers involved usually teach a large number of subjects, resulting in a low quality of education and little cross-fertilization of ideas. Most Bible schools do not offer academic accreditation, as their education standards do not meet internationally accepted

---

23. Ruaard Ganzevoort, "Myanmar Experiences" (unpublished report, Kerk in Actie, 2011), 10.

24. Salay Hta Oke, *Yangon Directory.* Also Lal Tin Hre and Samuel Ngun Ling, "Select Surveys on Theological Education in Emerging Asian Churches: Myanmar," *Ecumenical Review* (WCC) 64, no. 2 (2012): 75.

25. Ganzevoort, "Myanmar Experiences," 11–12; and Lal Tin Hre and Samuel Ngun Ling, "Select Surveys," 77.

26. The term "orphanage" is really a misnomer, as most of the children hosted in these homes have at least one parent. It would probably be better to refer to them as children's homes or hostels.

27. According to Lal Tin Hre, "some theological institutions in Myanmar are deeply dependent on external sources, on mission agencies and partners from abroad." Lal Tin Hre and Samuel Ngun Ling, "Select Surveys," 77.

benchmarks.[28] A third consequence of the widespread fragmentation is the limited availability of theological resources. Most libraries have only a limited selection of standard theological resources, and students often do not learn how to use these effectively.[29] Internet access is very limited or nonexistent, and students are not taught how to use electronic research resources.[30] Fourth, this fragmentation has often led to inadequate teaching methodologies. As discussed earlier, education in Myanmar has traditionally been based on learning by rote at the Buddhist monasteries. As Ngun Ling explains, this method focuses on acquiring knowledge by memorization, and it is still the predominant teaching style in basic education.

> Myanmar education and its teaching methodologies had been strongly influenced for centuries by [the] traditional Buddhist monastery teaching method known in Burmese as *kyet-thu-yueh sa-an*, meaning parrot learning method. This method is apparently monks' recital teaching method – a method of teaching in which pupils made oral response to or recitation of exactly what the monks or teachers taught or said. This kind of teaching methodology represents, in a sense, the monologue-style of teacher-student relationship in education. In this method, pupils have no right to question but recite only the words which the monks uttered to them. Either making a critical response or raising any question to the monk may mean to him insult or disrespect. Hence students who do not submit to this Buddhist culture may [have] action [taken] against them.[31]

As these monastic education methodologies have largely been carried over into theological education, it has led to teachers using "depository or banking methods rather than participatory methods in their teachings of theology. The

---

28. Only two institutions are accredited by ATA (MEGST & BTS; see www.ataasia.com), and ATESEA recognizes the degrees from eighteen affiliated colleges (cf. www.atesea.com).

29. Dawt Hlei Mawi, "A Comparative Study on the Development of Theological Institutes and Colleges Libraries in Yangon Division" (MA diss., Myanmar Evangelical Graduate School of Theology, 2010). Also Lal Tin Hre and Samuel Ngun Ling, "Select Surveys," 77.

30. "Lack of theological resources such as library and human resources including other technical materials is one of the major setbacks in promoting quality theological education in Myanmar. Most libraries of seminaries, theological colleges and Bible schools in Myanmar are not fully equipped with [an] adequate number of books in all theological disciplines," according to Ngun Ling, *Communicating Christ in Myanmar*, 127.

31. Ngun Ling, 126.

net result is that traditional teaching methods do not seem to help students learn and understand critically and creatively [what has] been taught."[32]

Finally, another weakness observed in theological education in Myanmar is a lack of contextualization. As a result of the high dependence on support from abroad, many theological institutions have simply replicated the standard curricula and teaching subjects from the donor countries or contexts.[33] In many cases this has led to indiscriminate importation of Western theologies, without much regard for the indigenous context and challenges.[34] Ngun Ling, advocating for a more critical level of contextualization, observes that

> not only the Baptists but also other Protestant Christians in Myanmar still follow verbatim the teachings of their Western missionaries. In fact, theological thinking that has prevailed among theological institutions run by more conservative churches [has] been and still [is] biblical-oriented and confessional, minimizing [the] relevance of the Christian message (the Word) changing socio-politico-economic and religious cultural contexts.[35]

While we may not necessarily subscribe to the author's understanding of contextualization, attention should be given to his observation that theological education in Myanmar needs to become more relevant and appropriate to the Myanmar context. Such a change in the approach to theological training may in turn lead to a more comprehensive transformation of the way the church in Myanmar reaches out beyond its boundaries.

The Church and the Challenge of Reconciliation

Ever since gaining independence from British rule, and most likely for many years before then, Myanmar has been plagued by internal strife. Although it is seventy years since independence, Myanmar is still experiencing armed conflict with several ethnic armed organizations, especially in the north and northeast

---

32. Ngun Ling, 126–27.

33. Ganzevoort, "Myanmar Experiences," 12.

34. Lal Tin Hre charges evangelical and fundamentalist schools with being particularly guilty of this practice. Lal Tin Hre and Samuel Ngun Ling, "Select Surveys," 77.

35. Ngun Ling, *Christianity through Our Neighbors' Eyes*, 190. Furthermore, "such imported forms of Western theological education have gradually dominated post-missionary theological education in Myanmar, weakening their connection with the practical, pastoral, and missiological concerns of local churches and also with new challenges of the contexts" (190).

of the country.[36] The roots of these conflicts have variously been identified as ethnic, religious, and identity issues. Mikael Gravers suggests that the cause is not primarily ethnic, but a prolonged postcolonial conflict between the military seeking to maintain the unity of the nation and minorities fighting for ethnic autonomy.[37] Elsewhere, however, he acknowledges that areas of friction over ethnic identity and nationalism have also been major drivers of the hostility, challenging the unity and harmony in the country:

> Ethnicity is one of the main ingredients and sources of cultural and political identification in the present world order. Ethnicity in its present forms is closely related to the modern development of nation states. However, it is also considered a source of conflicts and violence and one could often wish [that] ethnicity would altogether disappear from the political agenda, for example in Burma/Myanmar, a country long mired in ethno-nationalism and related conflicts and violence.[38]

In some ways these struggles for stronger ethnic autonomy are connected with the campaign to restore democracy to the country, which has sometimes overshadowed the cause of the ethnic minorities, especially in recent years.[39] Furthermore, religion is also considered an important dimension of the conflicts in Myanmar. Mikael Gravers alleges that under the military-aligned SPDC many Christian churches were closed when Buddhist people converted to Christianity. Also, Burmese troops have regularly demolished Christian crosses in Chin State and elsewhere. Muslims encounter widespread discrimination and violence, as mosques have been attacked and burned by Buddhist mobs.[40]

---

36. Cho Cho Myaing, "Forgiveness toward National Reconciliation in Myanmar from Christian Perspective" (MDiv diss., Myanmar Institute of Theology, 2013), 51.

37. Cf. Gravers, *Exploring Ethnic Diversity in Burma*, 8.

38. Gravers, *Exploring Ethnic Diversity in Burma*, 2: "Ethnicity is . . . an important source of self-identification, solidarity and empowerment in terms of belonging to a community and to a common culture and history – a source reinforced by migration and displacement."

39. "The nearly 60-year-long fight by Burma's ethnic minorities for autonomy and ethnic rights lies at the root of the country's broader political and humanitarian crisis. Yet, in the outside world, this issue is often subsumed under the better-known struggle for democracy, led by Aung San Suu Kyi and the National League for Democracy." Morten B. Pedersen, "Burma's Ethnic Minorities," *Critical Asian Studies* 40, no. 1 (2008): 45–66.

40. Gravers, *Exploring Ethnic Diversity in Burma*, 10.

Others maintain that religious conflict, although important, is not the most significant issue.[41]

Summarizing the conviction of many ethnic people in Myanmar, Cho Cho Myaing refers to David Steinberg's observations on the issues dividing the majority Bamar people from the other ethnic groups, claiming that the Burman people are prejudiced against the minorities and consider them to be less civilized.[42] According to Steinberg, the coercive power of the state is in the hands of the Burman leadership, and through its overwhelming dominance in the state and the military apparatus, the Burman leadership has used its power to further erode and reduce the autonomy of the minorities. Furthermore, although some autonomy for the minorities was retained under colonial rule and further promises were made under the first constitution (and the Panglong Agreement), this has never been fulfilled. Another grievance relates to the fact that the profits from exploitation of natural resources in minority areas have not been adequately shared and the minorities have been deprived of economic development. Finally, Steinberg alleges that the minorities have been denied the right to education in their native language.

Without speculating about which is the most relevant factor in the ongoing climate of conflict in the country, it is abundantly clear that Myanmar society continues to be highly polarized and fragmented. This is not the place to undertake a major investigation into the various causes and backgrounds of the different areas of friction in Myanmar society. Rather, the aim here is to consider the church's place and responsibility in this ongoing tragedy.

In this regard it may be illuminating to compare conditions in Myanmar with the situation in Malaysia. Peter Rowan, in his dissertation "Proclaiming the Peacemaker: The Malaysian Church as an Agent of Reconciliation in a Multicultural Society," examines the role the Malaysian church may play

---

41. See e.g. Ngun Ling, "Ethnicity, Religion and Theology in Asia," 6. "The misperceptions that have existed between the minorities and majorities seem to be by nature more racial and political than religious [when evaluated] from a historical perspective." Also, Cho Cho Myaing, "Forgiveness toward National Reconciliation," 51. However, not all observers agree, e.g. Philip Cope Suan Pau, "Peace Talk as Mission: Protestant Mission and Ethnic Insurgencies in Ethnocratic Buddhist Myanmar Today," 1, accessed 10 July 2017, https://www.academia.edu/19603279/Peace_Talk_as_Mission_Protestant_Mission_and_Ethnic_Insurgencies_in_Ethnocratic_Buddhist_Myanmar_Today. He sees it as "a religious conflict between Buddhism and Protestantism." Also, Aaron Tegenfeldt, "In Need of a Spiritual Framework for Peacebuilding: Burma and Beyond" (MA diss., University of Victoria, 2004), 34.

42. Cho Cho Myaing, "Forgiveness toward National Reconciliation," 56.

in overcoming the divisions in that society.[43] While there are significant differences in the religious, political, and social circumstances of the two countries, there are also some remarkable similarities. Referring to events surrounding the Japanese invasion of Malaysia during the Second World War, Rowan observes that the occupying Japanese gave preferential treatment to the majority population, while the minorities resisted the new imperial conquerors. He notes that, while mistreating the Chinese, the Japanese embraced a more pro-Malay stance, causing the Chinese to deeply resent the Malays. Similarly, in Myanmar the independence movement, led by Aung San, welcomed the Japanese as liberators from the British colonial administration, while most of the other ethnic groups opposed and resisted the occupation by the Japanese forces.[44] The opposing stances of these various ethnic groups in Myanmar were symptomatic of the hostility that has marked interethnic relations until now. Likewise, the identity of Malay Muslims is inextricably linked with Islam as their religion, in the same way that many in Myanmar consider Buddhism the axiomatic identity marker for the Bamar.[45]

A major portion of Rowan's research addresses the issue of how Christians can be faithful followers of Jesus, while at the same time being loyal citizens in a majority Muslim country. He asks:

> What role has the church played in working towards a united Malaysian community? How do Malaysian Christians approach the question of national identity? Given the social plurality of religions in its society, how can the church in Malaysia be committed both to the proclamation of the gospel and to being an agent for reconciliation in a divided country?[46]

He identifies three challenges for the churches in Malaysia. To start with, Christian churches are generally associated with the colonial past. Rowan points to the serious consequences of churches continuing to "cling on to patterns of Western or other non-indigenous forms of Christianity."[47] Second, Christian

43. Peter A. Rowan, "Proclaiming the Peacemaker: The Malaysian Church as an Agent of Reconciliation in a Multicultural Society" (PhD diss., Open University, All Nations Christian College, 2010).

44. This point has also been made by Matthew Walton in "Wages of Burman-Ness," 8.

45. Rowan points to "the inextricable bond made in Malaysia's Constitution between Malay ethnicity and Islam, so that to be Malay is to be Muslim. This is enshrined in Article 160 of the Federal Constitution of 1957: 'Malay is a person who professes the religion of Islam, habitually speaks the Malay language, conforms to Malay custom . . .'" "Proclaiming the Peacemaker," 122.

46. Rowan, 74.

47. Rowan, 132.

churches feel threatened by the steady process of Islamization. Rowan presents a list of restrictions on Christian activities which closely parallels the conditions in Buddhist Myanmar.[48] Third, the Christian church in Malaysia exists as a multiethnic community in a divided society. Rowan encourages the church to cultivate constructive relations with other ethnic groups, building trust relationships with followers of other religions, and demonstrating sensitivity in carrying out Christian evangelism and mission. He quotes Robert Hunt, who claims that "the Christian community is the only community in Malaysia that has no single dominant ethnic component, and which embraces all ethnic groups."[49] However, Rowan concedes that while the Malaysian church does bridge the ethnic divides, many churches are actually segregated, both locally and in their denominational structures.

Fundamentally, then, Christians in Malaysia face a monumental challenge:

> Even though the Malaysian church as a whole is inclusive of all ethnic groups, the segregation noted above suggests that ethnic identity is emphasised over and above membership of the global body of Christ. If this is indeed the case, it is certainly understandable in the light of Malay nationalism and the accompanying chauvinistic policies of the last forty years. In such a context non-Malay ethnic groups seek to strengthen their own cultural identity, each fearful of the dilution of their own ethnic distinctives.[50]

Despite the obvious differences, the Christian community in Myanmar shares many of the challenges identified in Malaysia. The association of the church with the colonial administration, the pressure of "Burmanization" on the Christian community, and the ethnic diversity of the church in a divided society: these have all been factors affecting the position and conditions facing the church in Myanmar. As in Malaysia, the Christian community needs to consider what role the church has played in working toward a united society in Myanmar, and how Myanmar Christians approach the question of national identity. Given the social plurality of religions in its society, how can the church

---

48. Göran Wiking, "Breaking the Pot: Contextual Issues to Survival Issues in Malaysian Churches" (PhD diss., Swedish Institute of Missionary Research, 2004), 77–78, cited in Rowan, 133.

49. Robert A. Hunt, "A Response by Robert A. Hunt," in Ng Kam Weng, *The Quest for Covenant Community and Pluralist Democracy in Islamic Context*, ed. Mark L. Y. Chan (Singapore: Trinity Theological College, 2008), 118, cited in Rowan, 137.

50. Rowan, 138.

in Myanmar be committed both to the proclamation of the gospel and to being an agent for reconciliation in a divided country? These questions will be more fully explored in chapter 4 ("Theological Reflection on the Church in a Pluralist Society"), but here we will briefly consider how the church has addressed this issue thus far.

Thus, the church in Myanmar faces two kinds of division. First, it is experiencing internal division along ethnic and denominational lines, and second, it is confronted by the larger separation between the different religions and ethnicities nationally. In order to engage the schisms in society at large, the church will first need to address its own divisions.

When surveying the Christian community in Myanmar, it does not take long to note the high number of Christian organizations and institutions, often separated along ethnic and linguistic lines. As we have seen, there are hundreds of Bible schools, seminaries, and training centers, and numerous orphanages across Myanmar.[51] The largest Protestant denomination, the Myanmar Baptist Convention (MBC), is divided along ethnic lines and most other churches (including nondenominational ones) also tend to attract members mostly from one particular ethnic group, whether or not this is reflected in the church name. Instead of demonstrating the heterogeneity of churches in this country, however, this diversity expresses their stratification, which has resulted in separating and isolating various ethnicities and faith traditions from one another. While it is undoubtedly easier for people from similar backgrounds to come together and build faith communities, there is beauty and fragrance in seeing individuals and groups from different cultures and ethnicities meeting together to worship the one God and Creator of all humankind.[52]

The second issue concerns the separation, at times spilling over into antagonism, between the different ethnicities in society. As the church is largely partitioned along ethnic lines, this also has an impact on how Christians relate to those from other ethnic groups. The problematic nature of interethnic relations therefore has serious ramifications for the missional role of the church.

Decades of ethnic strife have created an atmosphere of mistrust, bitterness, and alienation toward the dominant Bamar Buddhists.[53] Their nationalist

---

51. Salay Hta Oke, *Yangon Directory*.

52. The biblical and theological imperatives for this kind of spiritual unity will be further explored in chapter 4. Suffice it to note here the powerful message that is communicated by the spiritual unity of God's people, as also attested by the Lord Jesus in John 13:35: "By this everyone will know that you are my disciples, if you love one another." (Throughout this book, Scripture quotations are from the New International Version [NIV], unless otherwise noted.)

53. Gravers, *Exploring Ethnic Diversity in Burma*, 161, 251.

ideology, combined with religious supremacy, has left many Christians feeling betrayed and marginalized. Among Karen and Kachin believers in particular, many have strong feelings of bitterness toward the Bamar ethnic majority.[54] This strong resentment has created major obstacles for Christians to have a significant missional impact among their Buddhist fellow citizens. In the words of a Myanmar church pastor, "we need to acknowledge that these people need the Gospel, and we need to love them. But it took a long time for me to love them. I was honestly thinking, oh they don't go to heaven, praise the Lord! A lot of people are thinking that way."[55] Another pastor recounted hearing a Karen Christian announce, "When I go to heaven, I will look around, and if I find any Bamar people there, I would prefer to go to hell." Obviously, reconciliation – not only with God, but also with one another – is deeply needed, even among Christians.

---

54. Cockett, *Blood, Dreams and Gold*, 79, 84–85.
55. GCZ, interview with the author.

Part 2

Theological Reflection

3

Literature Review

This chapter will examine how various authors understand the basic nature of the church and what can be learned from these observations. Next, it will consider the mission of the church and its implications. Finally, it will explore how the church should function in a pluralistic world.

The Essence of the Church
The Community of Jesus: A Theology of the Church *edited by Kendell Easley and Christopher Morgan*

Easley and Morgan, editors of *The Community of Jesus*, refer to this volume as a "biblical, historical, systematic, missional journey" into the significance of the church.[1] According to the authors, the church is a community consisting of redeemed members (both Jew and Gentile; cf. Eph 2:11–22) with a centrifugal and centripetal mission. The church has a missional calling, both when gathered and when scattered.[2] In describing the nature of the church, they note that "the multinational nature of God's kingdom proclaims to the world that the God of Israel is not a tribal deity. He is the Creator, King, and Savior of the nations, and we will not know him in his full splendor until we know him as the King of the nations."[3] The first half of the book covers the biblical foundations of the church. The final four chapters build on this biblical core, connecting the theology of the church to church history, salvation history, God's glory, and God's mission.

---

1. Kendell Easley and Christopher W. Morgan, eds., *The Community of Jesus: A Theology of the Church* (Nashville, TN: Broadman & Holman, 2013), loc. 126, Kindle.

2. Easley and Morgan, *Community of Jesus*, loc. 5653.

3. Easley and Morgan, loc. 5657.

The Old Testament describes God's people as those who are on a journey with God. They respond to his call to faith through repentance and obedience, forming a kingdom of priests for God and for the world.[4] They are his people because God seeks, redeems, and gathers them.[5] As they gather, they form a visible community, demonstrating his greatness to the nations. In 2 Samuel 7:1–29, David's family is given a central role in God's redemptive plan, while Isaiah anticipates David's heir and ultimately a new creation for God's people gathered from among the nations (Isa 11:1–16; 65:17–66:24), as do 2 Corinthians 4:16–18 and Revelation 21:1–8. These passages show that the Old Testament people of God are one with his people in the New Testament and do not reveal an Israel versus the church dichotomy.[6]

Turning to the New Testament, the gospel writers present the Messiah and his kingdom, introducing a new messianic community, commissioned for the Messiah's mission. This community will extend beyond the ethnic boundaries of Israel to include the Gentiles. The mission of the Messiah will be carried out by his disciples in the power of the Holy Spirit (John 17:18; 20:21; see Luke 24:49; John 14:15–17; 16:7–11). This ministry will extend to all nations (Matt 28:19; see Gen 12:1–3). Acts (the birth of the church) and Revelation (its consummation) reveal that we are the people of God, the church of God, the servants of God, and the kingdom of God.[7] Paul's epistles deal with leadership structures in the church, its worship, and other practices. His writings make it clear that "the church exists not merely for itself but as a manifestation of God's grace in and for the world."[8]

In the General Epistles the church is consistently portrayed as the restored Israel, the new people of God (e.g. Heb 12:22–24). Believers are God's children and are thus brothers and sisters, making the church a family characterized by love.[9] In Hebrews the church is "the renewed Israel, heir of the promises of God rooted in Christ, set apart to him and holy, persevering in this world with an eschatological hope as it draws near to God."[10] In the Epistle of James the church is again the renewed Israel, a worshipping family created by God

---

4. Easley and Morgan, loc. 755.
5. Easley and Morgan, loc. 330.
6. Easley and Morgan, loc. 670.
7. Easley and Morgan, loc. 2280.
8. Easley and Morgan, loc. 2762.
9. Easley and Morgan, loc. 3372.
10. Easley and Morgan, loc. 3022.

to care for one another and to help one another to persevere.[11] In 1 Peter it is the new people of God, a loving family, rooted in Christ, distinct from the world, living in light of a future hope. In 2 Peter and Jude the church is the "set apart people of God, a family gathering regularly for a love meal and building one another up through prayer in the Holy Spirit and Scripture,"[12] defending the faith, holding fast, and awaiting the return of Christ. The church in John's epistles is striving to be a loving family united by God's love, pursuing holiness, and proclaiming Christ until he comes.

Looking at the church through the centuries, it is not difficult to observe that oftentimes, historical events, rather than theology, have influenced and directed its development.[13] The growing influence of the church facilitated its institutionalization, together with the expanding role of the clergy.[14] The schism with the church of the East was precipitated by the demise of the Roman Empire.[15] Even the Protestant Reformation did not originate from or result in a rethinking of the essence of the church, as most attention went to conflicts over soteriology and the role of the clergy.[16] The trend toward individualism from the Enlightenment era until now has been a more powerful driving factor in the emergence of new religious movements than any ecclesiological consideration or evaluation.[17] Thus, "the past highlights the inclination of Christian movements and denominations to absorb cultural influences into their ecclesiology. Institutional realities sometimes override scriptural principles in church life."[18]

Turning to theology, the author declares that "to understand the identity and nature of the church, we must view her in light of Jesus' person and work. For it is in Messiah Jesus that all the biblical covenants reach their fulfilment."[19] The church is the new covenant community, and as such it represents the one people of God throughout the ages. The church exists to display God's glory, through our union with Christ and with one another, based on our reconciliation through Christ's sacrifice on the cross. The final chapter focuses

---

11. Easley and Morgan, loc. 3085.
12. Easley and Morgan, loc. 3294.
13. Easley and Morgan, loc. 3606.
14. Easley and Morgan, loc. 3618–717.
15. Easley and Morgan, loc. 3719–818.
16. Easley and Morgan, loc. 3832–45.
17. Easley and Morgan, loc. 3974–99.
18. Easley and Morgan, loc. 3997.
19. Easley and Morgan, loc. 4605.

on God's mission which provides the "impetus, framework, and trajectory for the church's mission to glorify God among the nations."[20] The church does this by proclaiming the good news of God who redeems a people for himself. To understand the mission of the church, we need to recognize that it starts with God's mission. This mission begins with God as Creator, who forms man and woman in his image and intends them to live in relationship with God, with one another, with God's creation, and with themselves. However, the fall results in the need for redemption, which is accomplished by Christ and proclaimed by the church, his missional people:

> Articulated through the biblical narrative of creation, fall, redemption, and restoration, God's mission is to glorify himself by redeeming his image bearers and renewing his good creation, restoring them both to their intended shalom. God's mission provides the impetus, the framework, and the trajectory for the church's mission: to glorify God among the nations by proclaiming and promoting the good news that God is redeeming a people for himself and bringing all things under his good rule.[21]

Although not every author in this book focuses on the essence of the church, several conclusions can be drawn from this work. First, the basic continuity of God's engagement with humankind accentuates the unity of God's people throughout the Old and New Testaments. Second, God's plan of redemption is not only for the Jewish people, but encompasses all tribes, races, peoples, and nations. This is what makes the church truly universal, both in scope and in composition. Third, while the church does not replace Israel, it does constitute the fulfillment of God's design to create "a chosen people, a royal priesthood, a holy nation, God's special possession" (1 Pet 2:9). Finally, the church exists to glorify God among the nations by "proclaiming and promoting the good news that God is redeeming a people for himself and bringing all things under his good rule."[22]

While the universality of the church is asserted in several essays, there is only scant discussion of the implications of the all-inclusive nature of God's people. Particularly in an age in which racial and ethnic tensions and divisions are more prevalent than ever, it would have been helpful to confront this issue, which will be addressed in the next chapter. The Bible has much to say on

---

20. Easley and Morgan, loc. 5293.
21. Easley and Morgan, loc. 5671.
22. Easley and Morgan, loc. 5671.

the topic of managing diversity and overcoming discrimination within the community of faith, and the church is called to demonstrate this reconciliation both within its community and toward the world.

The Essence of the Church *by Craig Van Gelder*

"The church is. The church does what it is. The church organizes what it does."[23] These three short sentences, according to Craig Van Gelder, describe the essence of the church and point to its nature, ministry, and organization. Rather than defining the church in a functional way (in terms of its activities: what the church does) or in an organizational way (in terms of its structures: how the church is organized), Van Gelder suggests looking at what it means "to be the church."[24] He argues that it is critical to "consider the *nature* of the church before proceeding to define its *ministry* and *organization*."[25] Starting from a theological perspective, Van Gelder advocates a missional understanding of the church. According to this view, mission is not merely a function of the church, but rather points to its "essential nature."[26] He thus argues for a "missional ecclesiology" that understands the church as a "living community of God's people" as well as a "historical institution," while at the same time grounding mission in the "redemptive reign of the Triune God in all creation."[27] This is an important statement in that it affirms that the origin of mission is not in the church, but in God himself.

After a chapter dealing with historical developments, in which Van Gelder traces the understanding of the nature of the church through history, he turns to biblical perspectives on the church. He then puts forward one of his main propositions, namely that "the redemptive reign of God must serve as the foundation for defining the nature, ministry, and organization of the church."[28] In fact, he goes so far as to assert that misunderstanding the relationship between God's kingdom and the church is central to many of the problems

---

23. Craig Van Gelder, *The Essence of the Church: A Community Created by the Spirit* (Grand Rapids, MI: Baker, 2000), 37.

24. Van Gelder, *Essence of the Church*, 24.

25. Van Gelder, 24.

26. Van Gelder, 31. "Church and mission need to be merged into a common concept. Ecclesiology and missiology are not separate theological disciplines, but are, in fact, interrelated and complementary."

27. Van Gelder, 36.

28. Van Gelder, 74.

facing the church today.[29] This reveals one of his main concerns in the book, which is not primarily a theological concern, but a practical one. Van Gelder sees the church as God's community confronting the power of evil through his Spirit. Through its missionary nature, it takes part in establishing God's redemptive reign in this world. One should keep in mind, though, according to Van Gelder, that God's reign is not defined by the church; instead the role of the church is determined by God's reign.[30] Central to our understanding of church and mission is God's trinitarian nature, or, in Van Gelder's words, "the church is a relational community because God is a relational God."[31] One could say the Father's plan is that through creation, recreation, and consummation, the Son accomplishes the purposes and plans of the Father, while the Spirit implements the Father's plan and the Son's work.[32]

Next, Van Gelder examines the nature of the church. Drawing primarily from the book of Acts he concludes, "the church is a social community, a community made up of people who are reconciled with God and one another."[33] Then, returning to the historical descriptions of the church, he argues that it is not just holy, but also human (it is spiritual as well as social); it is both catholic and local (universal and contextual); it is both one and many (unified while at the same time diverse); and it is apostolic in the sense that it is not only foundational but also missionary (authoritative and sent).[34]

Moving to the ministry of the church, Van Gelder advocates making God's mission in the world our starting point, keeping in mind the communal nature of salvation.[35] God not only commits to a relationship with his people, but he intends to work through his people to bring salvation to the world, and thus the church is a "sign, foretaste, and instrument to invite all humanity and all creation to come to know fully the living and true God."[36] Stressing the corporate nature of the church, Van Gelder recommends emphasizing corporate spiritual formation rather than focusing on the individual. He identifies the following core ministry functions: worship (viewed as the central activity),

---

29. Van Gelder, 75.
30. Van Gelder, 87.
31. Van Gelder, 96.
32. Van Gelder, 97.
33. Van Gelder, 108.
34. Van Gelder, 116–26.
35. Van Gelder, 130.
36. Van Gelder, 139.

discipling, fellowshipping, serving, witness, visioning, and stewarding. All of these are rooted in the nature of the church.

The final chapter examines the organization of the church, as it provides the framework for its ministry. The structures of the church should be based on biblical foundations, building on historical developments, and reflecting contextual realities.[37] According to Van Gelder, the New Testament shows that local missional congregations were complemented by mobile missional structures, for example apostolic leaders, mobile teams, and at-large leaders, such as Philip, Apollos, and Priscilla and Aquila.[38] These mobile structures, although often operating autonomously, were still connected with and accountable to local congregations. When a conflict arose, the issue was addressed by a shared assembly (cf. Acts 15), and the outcome based on foundational beliefs and a shared contextual decision.[39] While local missional congregations live out God's redemptive purposes in specific contexts, mobile missional structures carry God's redemptive message to new areas. Both are necessary and require Spirit-filled leadership, which is described not only in terms of authority, but also as service, or ministry (*diakonia*).[40]

One valuable contribution of Van Gelder's book is the assertion that the church does not exist in and for itself. Rather, it serves to bear witness to God's redemptive reign in the world. As such, the church has both local and universal significance, enduring as well as dynamic structures, and both inward and outward ministries. Another point brought out by Van Gelder is the relational nature of God, and thus of the church. Salvation not only brings humankind back into fellowship with God, it also brings reconciliation to human relationships. As the title of the book indicates, Van Gelder focuses on the essence of the church. While he describes both the ministry and the organization of the church, his treatment of these topics in the final chapters remains somewhat superficial, thereby limiting the practical usefulness of this book in facilitating a thorough discussion of the church's nature, ministry, and organization.

For the purpose of this book, Van Gelder's work provides valuable insights regarding the church as a reconciled and reconciling community of God's people. Also, his depiction of the church as "sign, foretaste and instrument" of God's coming reign highlights the need to emphasize spiritual formation as a

---

37. Van Gelder, 159.
38. Van Gelder, 171.
39. Van Gelder, 177.
40. Van Gelder, 182.

corporate, rather than individual, obligation. This emphasis points to the need for the church to be both upward- and outward-focused, instead of just inward-focused. While these are valuable observations, Van Gelder unfortunately offers few concrete ways to apply these principles in the day-to-day life of the church.

The Mission of the Church
Transforming Mission *by David Bosch*

David Bosch's magnum opus has been recognized as a milestone in missiological studies and is widely acclaimed for its comprehensive scope and depth. Bosch states that the old paradigms of mission, referring to the sending out of missionaries and their activities or the agencies that sent them, are no longer valid.[41] This "crisis" in mission was caused by the fundamental changes that have swept the world since the end of the Second World War. Nevertheless, Bosch maintains that "Christianity is missionary by its very nature, or it denies its very *raison d'être*."[42] Mission is rooted in God and his relationship first with the people of Israel, and subsequently with God's people from all nations through faith in Christ Jesus. According to Bosch, evangelism as the proclamation of salvation through Jesus is an essential dimension of mission.[43]

Turning to the Bible, Bosch argues that mission in the traditional sense is not particularly prominent in the Old Testament.[44] Therefore he quickly moves to mission in the New Testament. The first change noticeable in the gospels is Jesus's inclusiveness. He not only reaches out to the marginalized, the downtrodden, and outcasts, but he also displays a remarkably positive attitude toward some non-Jews, such as the centurion in Capernaum and the Canaanite woman (Matt 8:10; 15:28). A second important feature is Jesus's announcement of God's kingdom or reign, as both a future and a present reality.[45] Third, Jesus's ministry was deeply intertwined with his disciples, who were called to be with him, to follow him, and to be sent out by him. Thus, discipleship and mission belong together and cannot be separated.[46] After Pentecost, as Jesus's followers began to spread out – either voluntarily or

---

41. David J. Bosch, *Transforming Mission: Paradigm Shifts in Theology of Mission*, 20th ed. (Maryland, NY: Orbis, 2011), 1.

42. Bosch, *Transforming Mission*, 9.

43. Bosch, 11.

44. Bosch, 18. While Israel is the center of attention, "there is an ambivalent attitude toward the other nations in the Old Testament."

45. Bosch, 32.

46. Bosch, 39.

because of persecution – new communities started to develop that were neither Jewish nor gentile, but comprised both. These heterogeneous communities were a living manifestation of the one body of Christ established by his death on the cross (Eph 2:14–16). Bosch observes that it sadly did not take long for the church to abandon its initial aspirations.[47] In the struggle for survival, its missionary calling was often superseded by a tendency to separate itself from others. In addition, the church "ceased to be a movement and turned into an institution."[48] Examining selected New Testament writers, Bosch concludes that for Matthew,

> Christians find their true identity when they are involved in mission, in communicating to others a new way of life, a new interpretation of reality and of God, and in committing themselves to the liberation and salvation of others. A missionary community is one that understands itself as being both different from and committed to its environment; it exists within its context in a way that is both winsome and challenging.[49]

This missional vitality is what made the early church such a dynamic movement that both conquered and transformed the first-century world around the Mediterranean.

A similar posture is found in Luke, where the church has both an inward and an outward orientation.[50] Just as Jesus has made peace between Jew and Gentile, so now his followers are sent into the world to be peacemakers.[51] Paul's writings further elaborate this idea by emphasizing that Christians find their identity in Jesus rather than in their particular race, culture, social class, or sex.[52]

In the next section Bosch turns his attention to understandings of Christian mission throughout history. He describes how the church – as it tried to determine its identity in a Hellenistic world – gradually and increasingly aligned itself with Greek philosophy and thought.[53] Nevertheless, Christians often distinguished themselves first and foremost by their conduct, revealing

---

47. Bosch, 45–47.
48. Bosch, 51.
49. Bosch, 84.
50. Bosch, 96.
51. Bosch, 120.
52. Bosch, 175.
53. Bosch, 199–200.

a higher morality than the surrounding society.[54] During the medieval period the church in western Europe shared authority with the state. This routinely led to the forced conversion of non-Christian peoples subjugated by Christian rulers, a practice which eventually extended to the Christianization of the areas colonized by Spain and Portugal, the two principal Christian nations.[55] At the same time a more benevolent missionary endeavor took place through the monastic movements spreading throughout the European continent.[56]

Moving to the Reformation period, Bosch outlines the main tenets of Reformed theology and discusses its impact on missionary thought and activity. It could be argued that the Reformation emphasis on the sovereignty of God tended to stifle any interest in, or motivation for, missionary engagement. In addition, the Protestant continuing belief in the connection between church and state resulted in a limited scope for missionary activity. Furthermore, internal rivalry among the various branches of the Reformation meant that little energy was left for outward initiatives.[57] It was through the influence first of Pietism, and then the Second Reformation and Puritanism, that Protestants began to give more thought to the importance of the missionary mandate.[58] These movements would later have a profound impact on the missionary efforts in the nineteenth and twentieth centuries.

Although the nineteenth century has been called the great missionary century, the Protestant missionary revival actually started earlier, in the eighteenth century.[59] While in some ways a response to the Enlightenment sweeping Europe in the preceding period, it nevertheless also carried many Enlightenment characteristics. Without claiming to be exhaustive, Bosch highlights a number of these, such as (1) an emphasis on the glory of God as missionary motive; (2) a constraint to reach out because of Jesus's love for every human being; (3) an often unacknowledged (or even unconscious)

---

54. Bosch, 217.

55. Bosch, 242.

56. Bosch, 235–39.

57. Bosch, 249. Bosch references Ursinus who argued that "obstacles to the conversion of pagans are insurmountable and the task is impossible; God has already made himself known to all nations, in various ways; the 'Great Commission' was for the apostles only and it is presumptuous on our part to arrogate it to ourselves; the pagan nations are, in addition, impervious to the gospel since many of them are savages who have absolutely nothing human about them."

58. Bosch, 262. E.g. Voetius advocated the conversion of the Gentiles and the planting of churches as demonstrations of divine glory and grace.

59. Philip Jenkins, *The Next Christendom: The Coming of Global Christianity* (New York: Oxford University Press, 2002), 52.

ethnocentrism on the part of the missionary; (4) the notion of manifest destiny, originating in the Enlightenment idea of Western superiority; (5) the protection and support received from colonial powers;[60] (6) a powerful eschatological motive for mission, whether pre-, post-, or amillennial; (7) the emergence of parachurch missionary societies; (8) a pragmatic, utilitarian disposition, emanating from an optimistic view of the future; and (9) an emphasis on the Great Commission (Matt 28:18–19) as biblical mandate for mission.[61] Overall, Bosch has a mixed view of this period, concluding that

> the entire Western missionary movement of the past three centuries emerged from the matrix of the Enlightenment. On the one hand, it spawned an attitude of tolerance to all people and a relativistic attitude toward belief of any kind; on the other, it gave birth to Western superiority feelings and prejudice.[62]

While tolerance toward others is surely to be applauded, there are probably more positive things to say about the accomplishments of missionary efforts during this era than Bosch acknowledges. Furthermore, one might question whether a relativistic attitude toward belief of any kind is something to be commended.

The cataclysms caused by two world wars and the end of centuries of colonialism prompt Bosch to identify one more "paradigm shift in mission." He points to how the Enlightenment rationalism and notion of continual progress gave way to the relativism and subjectivism of postmodern thinking.[63] The implications for Christian mission have been immense: in many countries, missionaries are no longer welcome. Even when they are still welcome, their role is more circumscribed and limited than before.[64]

Having carefully analyzed the many dimensions of mission throughout Scripture and across history, Bosch endeavors to synthesize its various understandings in the present. Even though the composite picture turns out

---

60. Bosch, *Transforming Mission*, 312. This led to the allegation that missionaries belonged to the three Cs of colonialism: Christianity, commerce, and civilization – in Myanmar better known as the three Ms: missionaries, merchants, and military.

61. Bosch, 292–349.

62. Bosch, 352.

63. Bosch, 360–66.

64. Bosch, 373. "It has become clear that the missionary is not central to the life and the future of the younger churches; in country after country (and especially in China) it has been demonstrated that the missionary is not only not central, but may in fact be an embarrassment and a liability."

to be both complex and often contradictory, he attempts to tie together some common strands.

First, mission and church are not subordinate to each other; instead, both are part of the *missio Dei*, and "the church changes from being the sender to being the one sent" for the sake of others.[65] In this paradigm,

> mission is not primarily an activity of the church, but an attribute of God. . . . It is not the church that has a mission of salvation to fulfil in the world; it is the mission of the Son and the Spirit through the Father that includes the church. . . . There is church because there is mission.[66]

Second, salvation should be seen in a holistic sense, encompassing the individual as well as the community, soul and body, both present and future.[67] Third, mission in this age must include both evangelism and social transformation.[68] Fourth, evangelism is integral to mission; it is a distinct part, but not separate from mission. It means "enlisting people for the reign of God, liberating them from themselves, their sins, and their entanglements, so that they will be free for God and neighbor."[69] Evangelism, according to David Bosch, includes many different aspects, from being set free from the world and its powers, to embracing Christ as Savior and Lord, participating with the church in the ministry of reconciliation, peace, and justice, and submitting to the rule of Christ over all things.[70] Fifth, while rejecting the excesses of Marxism-inspired liberation theology, Bosch nevertheless acknowledges the legitimate contemporary theologies that seek to address widespread social inequality and injustice.[71] Sixth, he argues for the need for unity in mission, or as he says "mission in unity,"[72] where ministry is carried out not only by the clergy, but by the whole church, laity and clergy together. Seventh, the existence of other religions necessitates dialogue, which must be done with an attitude of humility; it is, however, not a substitute for mission. Eighth, mission should be the theme of all theology, because just as "the church ceases to be

---

65. Bosch, 379.

66. Bosch, 400. Bosch attributes part of this quote to Jürgen Moltmann, *The Church in the Power of the Spirit: A Contribution to Messianic Ecclesiology* (London: SCM, 1977), 64.

67. Bosch, 409–10.

68. Bosch, 417.

69. Bosch, 428.

70. Bosch, 430.

71. Bosch, 453–56.

72. Bosch, 474.

the church if it is not missionary, theology ceases to be theology if it loses its missionary character."[73] Ninth, there is a complicated relationship between mission and eschatology. Quoting William Manson, Bosch argues that we need "an eschatology for mission which is both future-directed and oriented to the here and now."[74] It must hold together the already and the not yet; the future kingdom that has already come and the old world order that has not yet ended.

The concluding chapter of this book seeks to bring the different aspects of mission together in a comprehensive manner, encompassing "witness, service, justice, healing, reconciliation, liberation, peace, evangelism, fellowship, church planting, contextualization, and much more."[75] While incorporating all these elements in a definition may prevent a one-sided or distorted view of mission, Bosch himself may have fallen into the danger warned of by Stephen Neil's adage, "If everything is mission, nothing is mission."[76] In his effort to be balanced and inclusive, Bosch may have gone to the opposite extreme, trying to please everyone and thereby satisfying none.

His sixfold "faces of the church in mission" may be a more helpful proposition. It does not try to include every possible "missional" activity in a definition of mission, but rather looks at mission through the lens of six major "salvific events" in the New Testament: the incarnation, the crucifixion, the resurrection, the ascension, the coming of the Holy Spirit, and the parousia.[77] From these six events the following mission-related themes emerge: (1) The incarnation is a call to follow Jesus in genuine incarnational ministry. (2) The cross reminds us of the need for reconciliation, not just with God, but inevitably also with our enemies. (3) The resurrection is inseparable from the cross and a central element of the missionary message. (4) The ascension signals the arrival of God's reign on earth, and with it the need for kingdom transformation. (5) Pentecost tells us that God's mission can be done only in the power of the Holy Spirit. And (6) the parousia reminds us that the full realization of God's reign will be incomplete until the return of Jesus.[78] A shorter definition might be: mission is Christians participating in God's mission, sharing the love of Christ, incarnated in a witnessing community, for the sake of the world.[79]

---

73. Bosch, 506.
74. Bosch, 520.
75. Bosch, 524.
76. Bosch, 523. Quoted in the page preceding his broad definition.
77. Bosch, 524.
78. Bosch, 524–29.
79. Paraphrased from Bosch, 532.

For the purpose of this book, David Bosch provides several helpful observations: (1) the fact that mission is inseparable from discipleship;[80] (2) that the early churches in the diaspora formed heterogeneous communities, as a living manifestation of the one body of Christ;[81] (3) that these Christian communities were different from their surrounding society, and yet were committed to their environment, providing both an attraction and a challenge;[82] (4) that the Christians found identity in Jesus rather than in their particular race, culture, social class, or sex;[83] and (5) the affirmation that evangelism is wider than proclamation and covers different aspects, from being set free from the world and its powers to embracing Christ as Savior and Lord, participating with the church in the ministry of reconciliation, peace, and justice, and submitting to the rule of Christ over all things.[84] These insights will contribute to the missional model outlined in the following chapters.

The Mission of God's People *by Chris Wright*

Chris Wright's *The Mission of God's People* is a sequel to his much larger work *The Mission of God*. While the earlier book is a more comprehensive study of the mission of God from creation throughout history, Wright's present volume concentrates on the more limited topic of the mission of God's people "as they live in God's world and participate in God's mission."[85] Starting from the Lausanne Covenant statement that "world evangelization requires the whole church to take the whole Gospel to the whole world,"[86] he examines what should be understood by the "whole world," the "whole church," and the "whole Gospel." Wright contends that the church's mission is firmly rooted in God's mission, noting that "God's mission is for the sake of his whole world – indeed his whole creation. So, we have to start by seeing ourselves within the great flow of God's mission, and we must make sure that our own missional goals – long term and more immediate – are in line with God's."[87]

---

80. Bosch, 39.

81. Bosch, 48–49.

82. Bosch, 84.

83. Bosch, 175.

84. Bosch, 430.

85. Christopher J. H. Wright, *The Mission of God's People: A Biblical Theology of the Church's Mission*, Biblical Theology for Life (Grand Rapids, MI: Zondervan, 2010), 46.

86. The Lausanne Covenant came out of the first Lausanne Congress of Evangelism in 1974. https://lausanne.org/content/covenant/lausanne-covenant.

87. Wright, *Mission of God's People*, 26.

Wright rejects the tendency to narrow the scope of the gospel as if it only provides a solution to individual sin and offers entrance into heaven. Instead he strongly argues that the gospel message encompasses "the cosmic reign of God in Christ that will ultimately eradicate evil from God's universe."[88] Mission did not start with the Great Commission;[89] it is embedded in the biblical story from Genesis 1 through Revelation 22.[90] It includes a concern for the whole of creation.[91] The first missiological motif is God's covenant with Abraham, intended to bring blessing not only to him, but through him to all nations.[92] As we learn from Paul, this covenant not only is for Abraham's physical descendants, but through faith encompasses all of God's people.[93]

Genesis 18:19 brings together three important themes: God's choice of Abraham, Abraham's responsibility to walk in righteousness and justice, and God's promise to Abraham of blessing the nations. In this way, election, ethics, and mission come together in this one verse. In Wright's own words, "it is fundamentally a *missional* declaration, which *explains the reason for the election and explains the purpose of ethical living*."[94] In this way it provides an important link between ecclesiology and missiology.[95]

A second missional motif in the Old Testament is found in the exodus, which demonstrates that God will do "whatever it takes, to pay whatever it costs, in order to protect, defend and liberate his people."[96] The exodus provides a holistic model of redemption, encompassing political, economic, social, and spiritual dimensions, which requires an equally holistic understanding of biblical mission.[97] Such a holistic view of redemption calls for an equally holistic biblical model of "redemptive living" for God's people.[98] This template is found in the second half of the book of Exodus, with the giving of the law

---

88. Wright, 31.

89. Matt 28:19.

90. Wright refers to passages such as Gen 3; 12; Amos 9; and Isa 49. "God's mission is what spans the gap between the curse on the earth in Genesis 3 and the end of the curse in the new creation of Revelation 22." Wright, *Mission of God's People*, 46.

91. See e.g. Gen 1:26–28; 2:15; Ps 145; Isa 65:17–25; Hos 4:1–3; Rom 8:19–23; and Col 1:15–23.

92. Gen 12:1–3.

93. "What God promised to Abraham becomes the ultimate agenda for God's own mission (blessing the nations), and what Abraham did in response to God's promise becomes the historical model for our mission (faith and obedience)." Wright, *Mission of God's People*, 80.

94. Wright, 92 (italics original).

95. Wright, 93. "The church is missional or it is not church."

96. Wright, 99.

97. Wright, 102.

98. Wright, 108.

and the construction of the tabernacle.[99] As a kingdom of priests and a holy nation, Israel was called to bring God to the nations and the nations to God, in line with God's election of Abraham and promise to him. While holiness is not a precondition for salvation, it is a condition for mission.[100] Not only are God's people in the Old Testament called to represent God to the nations, they are also to live lives that attract others to the God who redeemed them and called them to holiness. According to Wright, this applies to Christians in the same way: "The world will be interested in our claims about God . . . only when it sees the visible evidence of a very different way of living."[101]

Like Abraham, God's people are chosen in order to serve him by being witnesses of the living God. Just as Israel was called to bear witness to God's uniqueness and sovereignty, so too are Jesus's followers. Even though present-day believers were not personally present at God's redemptive actions, in the Scriptures they have the testimony of those who were direct witnesses. The good news (*euangelion*) message found throughout the New Testament originates in the prophetic announcements of Isaiah announcing a return of the exiles[102] and the establishment of God's reign of peace and salvation. It is no surprise then that Jesus took one of these passages as the starting point of his mission (Isa 61:1–3), thereby proclaiming the arrival of God's reign. In speaking of the role of Jesus within this passage, Wright notes that "Christ is not only the messenger of good news (as per Is 52:7); Christ *is* the good news, in the sense that the gospel proclaims that Jesus of Nazareth is the Messiah – King and Savior – in fulfillment of the promises of God in all Scripture since Genesis."[103] This missionary (sending) mandate is found throughout the Bible, from Joseph in Genesis, to Moses, the judges, and prophets like Isaiah and Jeremiah.[104] This sending continues in the New Testament, with the Father sending the Son and the Spirit, and Jesus and the Spirit sending the apostles

---

99. In Exod 19:5–6 God challenges Moses and the Israelites, "Now if you obey me fully and keep my covenant, then out of all nations you will be my treasured possession. Although the whole earth is mine, you will be for me a kingdom of priests and a holy nation."

100. Wright points out how this missional idea is taken up and elaborated by both Paul (Rom 15:15–16) and Peter (1 Pet 2:9–12). Wright, *Mission of God's People*, 122.

101. Wright, 132. This attractional aspect of Israel's calling is further illustrated in 1 Kgs 8:41–43, 60–61 (the inauguration of Solomon's temple), Jer 13:1–11 (Jeremiah's waistband), and Isa 60:1–22 (worship of the nations).

102. Isa 40:9; 41:27; 52:7; 61:1.

103. Wright, *Mission of God's People*, 198 (italics original).

104. Cf. Gen 45:4–8; Exod 3:10–15; Judg 2:16; Isa 6:1–7; Jer 1:7.

("sent ones").[105] The primary task of the apostles was to bring the good news of God's kingdom to the nations,[106] although this did not exclude other ministries, such as taking care of the poor.[107] Wright points out that the role and title of apostle was not limited to the Twelve chosen specifically by Jesus.[108]

Nevertheless, the mission of God cannot be left to missionaries and other ministers of the Lord alone. God's concern encompasses the whole world of human productive and creative activity: trade, agriculture, industry, education, medicine, media, politics, government, sports, art, and entertainment.[109] All that happens in the public sphere of life, whether individually or corporately, is part of God's creation and therefore relevant to him. Although God is not necessarily pleased or glorified by everything that takes place in the public arena of life, he retains ultimate control. In the end, after the final judgment, all of creation will be redeemed and restored to its full glory.[110] As Christians we are called to be constructively engaged in the world and at the same time courageously confront the world where it stands against God. Wright contends that this is the challenge of being in the world but not of it, noting that "Christians are to be good citizens and good workers, *and thereby* to be good witnesses. Work is still a creational good. It is *good* to work, and it is good to *do good* by working. All this is part of the mission of God's people too."[111] In all likelihood, as the New Testament writers frequently declare, this challenge will include accepting suffering when confronting the idols of this world in one way or another.

Finally, the mission of God's people must include praise and prayer. Not only do we exist to glorify God, but we also live to bring others to worship and glorify him. Thus, God's people praying and praising the Lord is actually a way to bring his blessing to the nations, as they declare God's glory to them.[112]

---

105. John 3:17, 34; 4:34; 11:42; 17:18. Also Matt 15:24; Luke 4:18, 43; etc. On Jesus sending the apostles, cf. John 20:21.

106. "There is no doubt that the task of proclaiming the message of the gospel of Jesus Christ was the persistently top priority for the apostles." Wright, 213. See also Acts 20:24.

107. Acts 24:17. Wright notes how little attention is given in most commentaries to Paul's efforts to organize an offering for the poor in Jerusalem.

108. Cf. 1 Cor 15:7; Acts 14:14 (Barnabas); 2 Cor 8:23 (Titus); Phil 2:25 (Epaphroditus); Rom 16:7 (Andronicus and Junia); 1 Cor 12:28–29; Eph 4:11.

109. Wright, *Mission of God's People*, 222.

110. Wright, 227–28. Wright emphasizes that the earth will not be destroyed, but rather purged and purified.

111. Wright, 234 (italics original).

112. Wright, 251. "So we were *created* to bring glory to God our creator. We are *redeemed* to declare the praises of God to our redeemer" (italics original).

Wright has done the global church a great service with this book. He convincingly argues that the mission of God's people encompasses the whole world, including the importance of creation care and serving society. Furthermore, he exposes as false the dichotomies between individualistic and cosmic salvation, between faith and obedience, and between evangelism and social action. In his final comments he calls the church to rededicate itself to its biblical mission, to "go and make disciples," not merely converts. "The evangelization of the world, in the fullest sense of both the words in that phrase, remains as urgent a priority for the church as it was when Jesus laid it as a mandate on his disciples before his ascension."[113]

Wright emphasizes the continuity of God's mission in the world throughout history, and the need for integrating all aspects of life in the mission of the church. However, he pays less attention to the cultural diversity that characterized the early church, while all three themes are considered important here.

The Church in a Multicultural Context
Churches, Cultures and Leadership by Mark Lau Branson and Juan F. Martínez

Ever since its inception at Pentecost, the church has had to grapple with its relationship toward the cultures it engages with.[114] As a community that transcends ethnic and cultural boundaries, it has had to continually define its identity vis-à-vis the surrounding cultures. Mark Branson and Juan Martínez advocate a process of "reflective discernment" for church leaders in order to engage with the prevailing culture and to perceive the church's role in a multicultural context.[115] To this end they propose an interactive approach alternating between theory and praxis, based upon the educational theories of Paulo Freire. They suggest starting with identifying current praxis in the church and analyzing it, followed by a comprehensive study of Scripture, theology, and Christian history regarding such praxis.[116] This should generate conversations around personal and shared experiences related to these practices. This process should lead to discerning new ideas and praxis in accordance with the insights

---

113. Wright, 286.

114. Cf. Acts 6:1–7, where a conflict emerged between the Hebraic and the Hellenistic Jews.

115. Mark Lau Branson and Juan F. Martínez, *Churches, Cultures and Leadership: Practical Theology of Congregations and Ethnicities* (Downers Grove, IL: IVP Academic, 2011), 39.

116. Branson and Martínez, *Churches, Cultures and Leadership*, 42–44.

gained through the previous steps. This circular process should then be repeated in order to continually update praxis in line with both the unchanging truths of Scripture and the evolving realities of everyday experience.

A second major theme in this book concerns the role of leadership in the church. The authors advocate a threefold role for spiritual leaders, which they identify as interpretive, relational, and implemental leadership.[117] Through the first role, interpretive leadership, leaders help their community find meaning in their context and interpret this context for them. The second major theme, relational leadership, is about strengthening connections both within the church and with the surrounding community. Third, leaders need to be implemental in that they guide their community in launching new initiatives and developing new approaches in accordance with the needs of their community. The authors summarize this threefold role succinctly by stating that

> leadership is not about an individual or even a small group having great ideas and pulling a church into their vision. Leadership is about shaping an environment in which the people of God participate in the action-reflection cycle as they gain new capacities to discern what God is doing among and around them.[118]

While the church is a "sign, foretaste and instrument" of God's reign on earth, it also simultaneously finds itself in specific contexts.[119] The challenge for the church as a "contrast society" is to be aware of its context without allowing itself to be defined by it. A missional church needs to ask itself, "What is God doing in our context and how can we participate in his work?"[120]

In the authors' view, churches display the characteristics of communities by sharing memories and experiences, activities, and a common hope and imagined future, all of which are necessary components for discipleship and mission. This is even more important in congregations consisting of multiple ethnicities, where appreciation of one another's culture may lead to a better awareness and understanding of one's own culture. In such contexts it is vital to recognize the importance of people's worldviews, different language structures, and communication styles. The authors give various examples and illustrations from the United States to show the tensions between the majority (predominantly white) culture and minority populations, such as African-

---

117. Branson and Martínez, 55–56.
118. Branson and Martínez, 57.
119. Branson and Martínez, 66.
120. Branson and Martínez, 66.

Americans, Asian-Americans, and Latinos.[121] These tensions center on issues such as individual freedom versus mutual obligation, direct versus indirect problem-solving, formality versus informality, and competition and fair play. Intercultural skills are essential in order to navigate these conflicting values and approaches. Collectivist and individualist cultures can and should learn from one another:

> dominant-culture churches in the United States need to learn from minority churches about group harmony, cooperation and solidarity, recognizing that Western individualism often points us away from the biblical concept of the individual created by God to live in community. But those from individualist cultures can help believers from collectivist churches find the freedom of God's grace in Jesus Christ, something often missing in churches where the self is subsumed under the hierarchy of vertical leadership.[122]

The New Testament calls believers to live as redeemed individuals who find their identity and purpose in their relationship to God as they live in community. In the midst of this diversity, Christian leaders have a responsibility to guide their people through a reflective and interpretive process.

This "praxis cycle" consists of the five steps referred to earlier, starting with the present interpretation of Scripture (step 1) and how this has been shaped by one's culture and worldview (step 2). The initial understanding should be complemented by considering interpretations from diverse theological and cultural backgrounds (step 3). This may lead one to a deeper reflection on one's own biases (step 4) and to consider alternative viewpoints and interpretations (step 5).[123]

In the final section, Branson and Martínez move from the discussion of cultures to the role of leadership in the church. The authors suggest that leaders, using their interpretive skills, have a responsibility to lead the church in becoming aware of and interpreting the current environment of the church in order to help the community "make sense" of their situation.[124] As relational leaders, their task is to maintain stability and offer perspective amid the discomfort that is often the inevitable consequence of change.[125] At the

---

121. Branson and Martínez, 146–50.
122. Branson and Martínez, 166.
123. Branson and Martínez, 184–85.
124. Branson and Martínez, 190, 215.
125. Branson and Martínez, 217–18.

same time, leaders also need to create space for change experiments and other new initiatives, as this is part of the implemental role of a leader.[126] Branson and Martínez contend that, throughout this process, a missional leader must maintain the momentum for change, while at the same time safeguarding continuity.[127] Praxis-focused leaders shepherd their congregations through the phases of awareness, understanding, evaluation, and experimentation, toward commitment.[128] It is important to keep in mind that "leaders do not need to know the way – we just need the capacities to encourage and guide connections, to link Scripture and context, to engage neighbors and members, and to sanction questions and insights and innovations."[129] In the final chapter the authors point out that the process toward developing a multiethnic church usually starts with a culturally diverse leadership committed to move the church toward practices that reflect the heterogeneous nature of the community.[130] This will find expression in areas such as worship, preaching, prayer, hospitality, and decision-making. However, there is no single best approach for every situation, and a learning posture with discernment is the most important attribute.

Several findings by Branson and Martínez make significant contributions to the topic of this study. First, their description of the triple roles of leadership highlights the need for connection both within the church and with the surrounding community. Leaders need to guide their community in launching new initiatives that meet the needs of their community.[131] Second, they point out that a missional church should ask themselves what God is doing in their context and how they can participate in his work.[132] Third, those within multicultural churches should gain an appreciation of the cultures of others; this will lead to a better awareness and understanding of their own culture.[133] Fourth, the authors helpfully observe that developing a multiethnic church should start with a culturally diverse leadership committed to implement practices that support the heterogeneous composition of the church.[134]

---

126. Branson and Martínez, 221–22.

127. Branson and Martínez, 224.

128. Branson and Martínez, 226. These stages correspond to the reflective praxis model introduced earlier in the book.

129. Branson and Martínez, 231.

130. Branson and Martínez, 241.

131. Branson and Martínez, 56.

132. Branson and Martínez, 66.

133. Branson and Martínez, 146.

134. Branson and Martínez, 241.

Building a Healthy Multiethnic Church *by Mark DeYmaz*

This book is one of the earlier contributions to the topic of multiethnic churches. Mark DeYmaz does not offer a academic text, but rather a practical account of his own and others' experiences in forming a multiethnic church. He recounts the challenges in establishing Mosaic Church in Little Rock, Arkansas, some forty years after the city became known for its role in the desegregation of public schools in the United States. At the outset he points out that "Mosaic is not a church focused on racial reconciliation. Rather, we are focused on reconciling men and women to God through faith in Jesus Christ and on reconciling ourselves collectively with the principles and practices of local churches as described in the New Testament."[135]

In part 1, DeYmaz argues for a biblical foundation of unity within diversity for the church. First, he draws our attention to Jesus's prayer in John 17:

> that all of them *may be one*, Father, just as you are in me and I am in you. May they also be in us so that the world may believe that you have sent me. I have given them the glory that you gave me, that they *may be one* as we are one – I in them and you in me – so that they *may be brought to complete unity*. Then the world will know that you sent me and have loved them even as you have loved me.[136]

This threefold prayer for unity does not leave any doubt about the importance Jesus attaches to the unity of believers. What is perhaps less obvious is the reason for this prayer, namely to send a message to the world regarding God's love for them. DeYmaz concludes, "When men and women of diverse backgrounds walk together as one in Christ, they uniquely reflect the Father's love on earth as it is in heaven."[137]

Second, the book of Acts portrays the struggle of the early church to come to terms with the universality and inclusivity of the gospel.[138] From the God-fearing Jews from many nations mentioned in the Pentecost account, to Philip's ministry among Samaritans and to the Ethiopian eunuch, to Peter's reluctant visit to the gentile Cornelius: each of these narratives accentuates the barriers that needed to be crossed as the gospel began to extend ever further from

---

135. Mark DeYmaz, *Building a Healthy Multi-Ethnic Church: Mandate, Commitments and Practices of a Diverse Congregation* (San Francisco: Jossey-Bass, 2007), loc. 457, Kindle.

136. John 17:21–23 (italics added).

137. DeYmaz, *Healthy Multi-Ethnic Church*, 9.

138. DeYmaz, 14.

its origins in Jerusalem.[139] However, when Luke describes the leaders of the church in Antioch, it is noteworthy that he specifically mentions their diverse cultural backgrounds.[140]

Third, DeYmaz turns to the apostle Paul and his letter to the Ephesians. The church there, he notes, was composed of believers from both Jewish and Greek backgrounds.[141] This is reflected in Paul's vision for the church, which is to be "an authentic, visible community of faith where people of diverse backgrounds worship God together as one, and love one another in Christ."[142] It is also the essence of the mystery, as Paul describes it, "that through the gospel the Gentiles are heirs together with Israel, members together of one body, and sharers in the promise in Christ Jesus" (Eph 3:6). This oneness will flourish in a loving, inclusive community, where believers from Jewish and gentile backgrounds meet together at the cross. In the local church, all believers, no matter who they are or where they come from, are one family, with one Father, to the glory of God.[143]

In part 2, DeYmaz suggests seven core commitments a church needs to make in order to be(come) truly multiethnic: they need to embrace dependence, take intentional steps, empower diverse leadership, develop cross-cultural relationships, pursue cross-cultural competence, promote a spirit of inclusion, and mobilize for impact.[144] He traces his own journey through these seven principles, detailing the many challenges he and his church faced while going through this process. In part 3 he introduces two more examples of multiethnic churches, described in separate chapters by those involved with them. One of these was a declining homogeneous church on its way to extinction, which was revitalized through its transition to a more multiethnic community. The other church, formerly monocultural and white, was challenged by visitors to transform into a more diverse and inclusive community. The authors are honest in acknowledging the challenges they faced in the process of

---

139. DeYmaz, 16–17. Noting that the ethnicity of the Samaritans and of an Ethiopian who believed in Christ is mentioned, DeYmaz argues that this shows that the gospel is not just for Jews.

140. Acts 13:1. Barnabas was born in Cyprus (Acts 4:36–37); Simeon, as his nickname Niger indicates, probably came from Africa; Lucius was from North Africa (Cyrene); Manaen, through his association with Herod, may have been brought up either in Rome or somewhere in Palestine; and Saul was a native of Tarsus in Asia Minor.

141. DeYmaz, *Healthy Multi-Ethnic Church*, 28.

142. DeYmaz, 29.

143. DeYmaz, 33.

144. Part 2, chapters 4–10. DeYmaz, 43–129.

transitioning, such as resistance from the original members of the church, ignorance and insensitivity on the side of more conservative members, and problems integrating new believers from widely different ethnic and cultural backgrounds, many of whom came from dysfunctional and broken families.[145]

Throughout his book Mark DeYmaz gives innumerable practical suggestions. For example, multiethnic church planters do not have to be experts in the language, culture, or customs of each people group.[146] More important is to humbly engage each culture in the church with respect.[147] Since cross-cultural competency and mutual respect are crucial for the ministry leaders in seeking to understand and resolve cultural differences,

> forging unity from diversity will require transformational leaders of diverse ethnic background to come together as one. All involved must passionately embrace the vision in order to lead the people with whom they have the greatest influence. There can be no hint of inconsistency, self-positioning, or diversion from the vision if it is, in fact, to take root and inspire change in the established church.[148]

The examples and illustrations demonstrate that establishing a multiethnic church, either from scratch or transitioning from an existing congregation, is a major undertaking, with numerous pitfalls and obstacles. Yet the biblical challenge remains that Christ came to

> create in himself one new humanity out of the two, thus making peace, and in one body to reconcile both of them to God through the cross, by which he put to death their hostility. He came and preached peace to you who were far away and peace to those who were near. For through him we both have access to the Father by one Spirit. (Eph 2:15–18)

While it may certainly be easier to establish and lead a monocultural church, the challenge from Scripture to bring together different communities remains. The gospel has clear implications for how we relate to one another, and calls us to be peacemakers and bridgebuilders, striving to unite people from different communities within the one body of Christ. While the author offers compelling biblical arguments and solid practical suggestions for establishing

---

145. DeYmaz, 136.

146. DeYmaz, 136–46.

147. DeYmaz, 143.

148. DeYmaz, 179.

multiethnic churches, it should be acknowledged that he is addressing a North American audience, where churches are found among different ethnic communities already. In Myanmar, where large areas of the country are dominated by the Bamar Buddhist majority, it may be much more difficult to engage in meaningful multiethnic ministry. This model may therefore be more suited to urban areas, where different ethnicities are living together and mingling with each other.

Christianity through Our Neighbors' Eyes *by Samuel Ngun Ling*

Having considered primarily Western authors so far in this literature review, it is important to give voice to a theologian from Myanmar regarding the impact and challenges of mission work in this country.[149] Samuel Ngun Ling is a professor of Systematic Theology and president of the Myanmar Institute of Theology (MIT). He has written several books and articles on interfaith dialogue and communication of the gospel, specifically in the Myanmar context.[150] Tracing the history of American Baptist mission work in Myanmar and the obstacles encountered during that period, Ngun Ling takes a dim view of approaches by both foreign missionaries and some of their local counterparts, as illustrated in the foreword, where he notes that Christianity from the start was associated with the "imperialistic actions of colonizers."[151] He explains that "to a Burman, embracing a foreign faith therefore almost means ceasing to be a Burman."[152] Thus, for a Burman to become a Christian is seen as being a disloyal citizen, or more precisely, becoming like a foreigner. Furthermore, since Christianity is more generally accepted by the ethnic minorities, who are regarded as inferior by the Burmans, it is difficult for Burmans to accept this minority religion.[153]

Ngun Ling identifies the following perceptions of Christianity during the missionary (colonial) era. Christianity was seen as an inferior foreign, and

---

149. Even though most authors evaluated here may be considered Western, some of them do demonstrate a more global perspective, such as Branson and Martínez, and DeYmaz.

150. E.g. Ngun Ling, *Christianity through Our Neighbors' Eyes*; Ngun Ling, *Communicating Christ in Myanmar*; Ngun Ling, "Doing Theology under the Bo Tree: Communicating the Christian Gospel in the Bama Buddhist Context," in *Called to Be a Community: Myanmar's in Search of New Pedagogies of Encounter: The First Seminar of Myanmar Theologians*, conference publication (private circulation), ed. Samuel Ngun Ling, Than Win, and Peter Joseph (Yangon: Association for Theological Education in Myanmar, 2003), 171–84.

151. Ngun Ling, *Christianity through Our Neighbors' Eyes*, page d.

152. Ngun Ling, 45.

153. Ngun Ling, 51.

even colonial, religion, and thus a political threat to the Buddhist kingdom.[154] From 1886, when the whole of Myanmar became subject to the British, Christianity was perceived as the British colonial religion, since it removed Buddhism as the state religion and replaced Buddhist monastery education with the British secular and American missionary educational systems, while giving special protection or patronage to Christianity.[155] He argues there is fundamental suspicion in Myanmar with regard to Christianity, which is seen as an imperialistic ethnic minority religion, and as a betrayer of Burmese Buddhist culture and social life.[156]

Once the colonial period ended and Burma regained its independence, the roles of the religions were reversed again, and Buddhism reclaimed its privileged position. "This *special status* of favored religion tends to minimize the freedom of other unfavored religions, those which do not have *special status*, although the government claims to embrace all religions to flourish together peacefully and harmoniously."[157] However, in 1966 all foreign Christian missionaries and administrators were forced to leave the country, and since then, freedom of religion has existed more in theory than in practice, so that strict rules are set and permission required for Christian meetings, conferences, evangelistic campaigns, building churches, and publications.[158] Among the consequences of this (Buddhist) prejudice has been discrimination against adherents of other religions in the country, and, consequently, an identity crisis when an ethnic Burman Buddhist becomes a Christian.[159] This is based at least partly on the perception that when a Burman Buddhist becomes a Christian, he or she is being disloyal to the Buddhist society.[160] According to Ngun Ling, it was primarily British colonization, not Christian mission, which made Christianity culturally alien and sociopolitically undesirable for typical Burman Buddhists.[161]

When attempting to address these biased perceptions, it should be noted that, while understanding ethnic Christianity is important for majority

---

154. Ngun Ling, 45–62.
155. Ngun Ling, 56.
156. Ngun Ling, 62.
157. Ngun Ling, 124–25 (italics original).
158. Ngun Ling, 159.
159. Ngun Ling, 161.
160. Ngun Ling, 161.
161. Ngun Ling, 162.

Buddhists, it is even more necessary for ethnic minority Christians to take seriously Buddhist issues such as their doctrines, worldviews, and behaviors.[162]

Ngun Ling observes that Baptist principles and doctrines are predominantly Western-oriented, especially with regard to the church, such as forms of worship and church organization (ecclesiology), the expression of God and salvation (theology), and concepts and strategies of mission outreach (missiology).[163] He then suggests that "contextualization requires of the Baptist and other Christian Churches to deconstruct all Western thought forms, Western forms of worship, and Western structures of the churches, and at the same time to reconstruct them in [a] Burmese way and thought forms with the use of Burmese religious and cultural resources."[164] According to him, the American Baptist Mission (commonly known as the American Baptist Foreign Mission Society) divided people along racial and cultural lines, so that they became separated, not only from each other but also from the larger Buddhist society.[165] Furthermore, "because of their exclusive Christian mentality and *holier-than-thou* attitude, very little attention is being paid to the questions and challenges posed by people of other faiths in present-day Myanmar."[166]

Considering how to address these communication challenges, Samuel Ngun Ling attributes the failure of Christian mission among Burman Buddhists to its teaching and presentation methods. He charges Myanmar Christians with uncritically copying Western missionary approaches, thereby "minimizing [the] relevance of the Christian message," and argues that "imported forms of Western theological education have gradually dominated post-missionary theological education in Myanmar, weakening their connection with the practical, pastoral, and missiological concerns of local churches and also with new challenges of the contexts."[167] His view is that "a theology in Asia must be a theology that is rooted or planted in Asian ethnic/tribal soil, so that it grows out of rich Asian cultural fertility so as to bear distinctive fruits for Asia and the world."[168] Concerning the role of theology and mission, he adds, "A living theology in Asia must speak to the actual questions men and women are asking in the midst of their dilemmas and hopes; aspirations and achievements;

---

162. Ngun Ling, 177.

163. Ngun Ling, 128.

164. Ngun Ling, 129.

165. Ngun Ling, 132.

166. Ngun Ling, 130 (italics original).

167. Ngun Ling, 190.

168. Ngun Ling, 192.

doubts, despair, and suffering."[169] Referring to Myanmar's long history of conflict and fighting for freedom from oppression, Ngun Ling comments that these conflicts have perpetuated hatred and animosity between the majority Buddhists and the minority ethnic peoples of Myanmar until now. His question is, "How to build a peaceful society in Myanmar? How can inflicted [*sic*] or oppressed peoples become good neighbors to each other? Peoples can forgive, but many can never forget the history."[170]

While Ngun Ling's concern regarding the negative impact of Western (colonial as well as postcolonial) practices and methodologies is justifiable, it may be all too convenient to attribute today's challenges entirely to colonial-era missionaries and their present-day followers. After all, more than fifty years have passed since all missionaries and mission agencies were expelled from Myanmar, and the church has developed and matured substantially since then. The subsequent isolation of the country in the following decades and the tendency to maintain customs and traditions may equally have played a part. In addition, while Ngun Ling rightly focuses on the need to know and understand the religious beliefs and practices of the Buddhist majority in the country, his primary aim seems to be fostering mutual acceptance and understanding, given his emphasis on peacebuilding and interreligious dialogue. The gospel certainly advocates reconciliation and interethnic harmony, but these cannot be detached from spiritual transformation through the life-changing power of the Holy Spirit, both within individuals and in the Christian community. His endorsement of religious dialogue leads him to contend that truth is relative and therefore no religion should make exclusive claims over against other religions.[171] However, genuine cross-cultural communication of the gospel should go further than merely promoting interreligious harmony. Mission (of which cross-cultural gospel communication is one aspect) is concerned with spiritual transformation as an expression of the kingdom of God in individuals, families, and communities. Since this is particularly relevant in pluralist environments, the next chapter will focus on how the church can carry out its mission in a pluralist society such as Myanmar.

---

169. Ngun Ling, 218.

170. Ngun Ling, 249–50.

171. Ngun Ling, 283. He approvingly quotes the Buddha's illustration of six blind men describing an elephant. None of them possessed an accurate, complete view of the animal. Therefore, he argues, "none of us is able to grasp the final or absolute truth. Truth is thus profoundly mysterious, relative, and universal [so] that no one can claim monopoly of it."

4

Theological Reflection on the Church in a Pluralist Society

This chapter lays the theological foundation for a biblical understanding of the church as a diverse but unified body of redeemed people. Several key Bible passages focusing on the significance of this reality will be examined. This understanding is essential for the church in Myanmar to fulfill its mandate to be a missional body, demonstrating God's love in a fractured multiethnic society. Several challenges to fulfilling this role will be examined, together with various initiatives that may lead toward reconciliation and diversity within the church and in society.

Understanding the Essential Characteristics of the Church
The Church Is One Body in Christ (Rom 12:3–8)

Of all the New Testament images of the church, one of the most powerful is Paul's portrayal of the church as the body of Christ (Rom 12:5). While Jesus spoke about his body on several occasions, it was always in reference to his physical body in connection with the Last Supper (Matt 26:26; Mark 14:22; Luke 22:19). Therefore, Paul was breaking new ground when he introduced the image of the church as the body of Christ. While the idea of a community of people as a body was not unknown in the apostolic era, it was Paul who applied it specifically to the church as a community.[1] In 1 Corinthians 10:16 and 11:29, Paul speaks of the body of Christ to refer to the sacrament of the cup and bread,

---

1. Van Gelder, *Essence of the Church*, 110. The image of a sociopolitical group as a body was not uncommon in the first century. Paul, however, was the first to apply this image specifically to the church as Christ's body in the world. Also see Craig S. Keener, *Romans*, New Covenant Commentary Series (Eugene, OR: Cascade, 2009), 145.

concluding that "because there is one bread, we who are many are one body, for we all partake of the one bread" (10:17 ESV). Thus, Paul uses this image to emphasize the essential unity of the church as forming one body. Similarly, in Romans 12 he employs the same image to contend for the unity within the body of Christ (the church) in all its diversity. While acknowledging that Christians are different members, each with their own individual functions, he insists that together they form one body in Christ (12:5). Moreover, Paul adds that "individually [they are] members one of another" (12:5 ESV). This unity in diversity connects the members first to Christ, and then to each other. Paul further develops this concept of unity in diversity by connecting it with the gifts of the Spirit, which are apportioned "according to the grace given to us" (12:6 ESV).[2] Craig Van Gelder affirms this, saying, "The nature of the church entails an interdependence among all the members. This interdependence is a function of the diversity of spiritual gifts that have been given by the Spirit for ministry by members."[3] It seems significant that Paul repeatedly addresses this issue of recognizing the unity of the body in the face of diversity within congregations. Here in Romans he urges each believer to "not think of yourself more highly than you ought" (12:3), obviously because some members were tempted to look down on others.

In 1 Corinthians 12, Paul addresses the same issue from two different angles. First, he speaks to those who feel overlooked, as if they do not belong to the body (12:15–16). Next, he confronts those who consider themselves superior and want to exclude others whom they deem less important or less valuable (12:17). He then makes it clear that "God has placed the parts in the body, every one of them, just as he wanted them to be" (12:18). There is, therefore, in Paul's opinion, no excuse for excluding either oneself or others from the body of Christ. All members are valuable and indispensable. It is probably no coincidence that the passage on the body of Christ in Romans is wedged between Romans 12:1–2, which speaks of offering our bodies as a living sacrifice and "not conform[ing] to the pattern of this world, but be[ing] transformed by the renewing of your mind," and Romans 12:9–21, which challenges believers to "be devoted to one another in love. Honor one another above yourselves" (12:10).

Clearly the church as the body of Christ is not a uniform, homogeneous group of people. However, there is a basic foundational unity, which is organic and integrated, a unity in diversity. This heterogeneous, or composite, unity is

---

2. Keener, *Romans*, 145.

3. Van Gelder, *Essence of the Church*, 110.

what enables the church to display "the manifold wisdom of God" (Eph 3:10) to this world.[4] Through reconciled relationships and mutual submission church members can experience true oneness within the body of Christ without losing their uniqueness.

Christ Has Removed the Barriers (Eph 2:11–22)

At first glance it may seem that Ephesians 2 addresses similar themes to those found in Romans 12, namely the unity of believers in the church. However, Paul here approaches the subject from a very different perspective. Although he does speak about Jewish and gentile Christians being brought together through Christ, he employs other ideas besides "one body." Here he emphasizes the image of "one new man in place of the two" (2:15 ESV), of coming together in one household (2:19), and of being built into a temple (2:21).

First, however, Paul focuses on the fact that non-Jews used to be "separate from Christ, excluded from citizenship in Israel and foreigners to the covenants of the promise, without hope and without God in the world" (2:12). As uncircumcised people they were outsiders and had no prospect of fellowship with God. Paul does specify that he is talking about the outward circumcision "in the body" (v. 11), thereby indirectly acknowledging that what really matters is circumcision of the heart.[5] Verses 14–18 form a parenthetical section, focusing on the peace and reconciliation brought by Jesus Christ, after which Paul resumes the theme of the Gentiles no longer being "excluded . . . and foreigners." But first, in verses 14–18, he elaborates on Jesus as Peacemaker, who has broken down the dividing wall of hostility that stood between Jews and Gentiles (2:14).[6] According to Leslie Mitton, this wall of hostility should be interpreted metaphorically as an attitude of the heart "which holds apart whole

---

4. Paul extends this to "the rulers and authorities in the heavenly realms." According to C. Leslie Mitton, former divisions are healed in the church through Christ's reconciling power, bringing unity and peace in place of hostility; cf. C. Leslie Mitton, *Ephesians*, New Century Bible Commentary (Grand Rapids, MI: Eerdmans, 1989), 126. Perhaps a more vivid way of expressing this would be to speak of the multicolored wisdom of God.

5. In Rom 2:29 he makes this explicit when he says that "a Jew is one inwardly, and circumcision is a matter of the heart, by the Spirit, not by the letter" (ESV).

6. Some commentators argue that this "dividing wall" is a reference to the division that existed in the temple between the temple proper and the Court of the Gentiles. Cf. Francis Foulkes, *Ephesians*, Tyndale New Testament Commentaries 10 (Downers Grove, IL: InterVarsity Press, 2008; Olive Tree Bible Study Digital Edition), on Eph 2:14. This possibility is also mentioned by James D. G. Dunn, *Romans 1–8*, Word Biblical Commentary 38a (Dallas: Word, 2012; Olive Tree Bible Software), although he rejects it in favor of seeing the fence as a reference to the law.

communities of people in suspicion and hatred of one another. . . . It was this hostility, firmly implanted in human hearts, which Christ had melted away, so that Christians, whether Jewish or Gentile, found themselves knit together in a new and unbelievable friendship."[7] The result is that Christ created "one new humanity out of the two," thus reconciling the two both to God and to one another, thereby removing ("putting to death") the hostility (vv. 15–16). This act of creating a new community, by incorporating former enemies, is further elaborated in verse 17, where Paul underscores that Christ has brought peace both to "you who were far away" (the Gentiles) and "to those who were near" (the Jews). The next verse makes it even clearer that there is no more distinction between the two groups, "for through him we both have access to the Father by one Spirit" (v. 18). Clearly in God's new humanity there is full equality among believers, whatever their background.

After this short intermezzo Paul continues on from the topic addressed in verses 12–13, the end of alienation and separation of the Gentiles. In verse 19 he announces to the gentile believers, "you are no longer foreigners and strangers, but fellow citizens with God's people and also members of his household." This is an extraordinary declaration in view of their traditional separation from the Jewish people. From now on they belong together in one house, a building that "rises to become a holy temple" (v. 21). In verse 20, Paul develops the image even further. Not only do the believers together form a temple, but in Christ they are also "built on the foundation of the apostles and prophets, with Christ Jesus himself as the chief cornerstone." Paul's theology is both groundbreaking and thoroughly trinitarian. It establishes that God has expanded his covenant with Israel to include all nations, regardless of ethnic origin or circumcision or non-circumcision, and even without regard to prior compliance with the law, as Paul asserted in verse 15. By the blood of Christ, God has established a new humanity, a spiritual community. Elsewhere he elaborates by saying that "through the gospel the Gentiles are heirs together with Israel, members together of one body, and sharers together in the promise in Christ Jesus" (3:6). Instead of being an exclusive single ethnicity, the church is meant to be an open, inclusive, welcoming multiethnic community, held together by Christ, its head and cornerstone.

---

7. Mitton, *Ephesians*, 105. Dunn further specifies that this "fence" refers to the law which "in functioning as a fence to protect Israel from the impurity of the Gentiles . . . became such a sign of Jewish particularism that it also alienated Gentiles and became a cause of hostility." Dunn, *Romans 1–8*, on v. 15.

A Message of Unity to the World (John 13:34–35)

The previous two passages have helped to determine the essence and composition of the church according to the apostle Paul. Turning to Jesus's view of the church, it is noteworthy to observe that he is not primarily concerned with its nature or internal makeup, but more specifically with how it should function in everyday life. Shortly before his arrest and trial, Jesus spent the last few hours among his disciples, preparing them for living in a new kind of community that was to have a profound impact on the world (John 13–17). After telling his disciples that he would not be with them much longer, he changed the topic of the conversation, saying, "A new command I give you: Love one another. As I have loved you, so you must love one another. By this everyone will know that you are my disciples, if you love one another" (John 13:34–35). This is the first of two instances when Jesus commanded his disciples to love one another, the other being in 15:12. However, only on this occasion does he refer to it as a "new" command. In the Old Testament the people of Israel had received the command to "love your neighbor as yourself" (Lev 19:18), but here the disciples were told, "As I have loved you, so you must love one another." This added a new dimension to the old commandment, and thus it is described as "new." The new love that should characterize relationships among the disciples (who had been fighting not long before about who should be first) is defined by Jesus's own love for them (cf. John 13:34; 15:9, 12). This love was to lead Jesus to lay down his life for them, and here he commanded them to love one another in the same way.[8]

The importance of the disciples' love for one another is evident in Jesus's explanation in the following verse: "By this everyone will know that you are my disciples, if you love one another" (13:35). It must be noted that this verse does not indicate the reason why the disciples should love one another. Rather, their love for one another would bring the outside world to recognize that they were indeed true followers of Jesus, as Colin Kruse observes in his commentary on this verse:

> People would be able to recognize them as Jesus' disciples by their mutual love. Knowing the truth about Jesus is vital, but so also is believers' love for one another. This love is not sentimental, but real self-sacrificing love by which they place other believers'

---

8. It is clear that the message eventually did get through to the disciples, as evidenced in 1 John 3:16: "This is how we know what love is: Jesus Christ laid down his life for us. And we ought to lay down our lives for our brothers and sisters."

needs above their own. Lovelessness among believers nullifies their witness to the world, and reveals them as hypocrites.[9]

It also bears pointing out that Jesus's words "as I have loved you" do not primarily refer to his death on the cross – which had not yet taken place at that point – but to his very practical and specific act of love: the washing of the disciples' feet earlier that evening. This demonstration of selfless love and humility would undoubtedly still have been fresh in their memory. Jesus's command, therefore, implies that "to truly love another, we must pursue a life of servanthood and sacrifice."[10]

For Christians to merit the attention of the world, they need to take Jesus's command to heart, laying aside petty squabbles and obeying his exhortation to love one another unconditionally. Only a sincere desire to follow Jesus in sacrificial love can cultivate a unity that will send a message to the world. This love must embrace and include people from every ethnicity, language, culture, and nation. It must include those who are despised and rejected by society, as well as those who have caused suffering for others. Only then will the church be the inclusive community God intended it to be, and only then will the church be able to draw in those who are hungering and thirsting for authentic love and life.[11]

Recognizing the Importance of Reconciliation

One significant outcome from examining the nature of the church within a biblical perspective has been to recognize its intrinsic unity within vast diversity.[12] The church was established to bring together Jews and Gentiles, slave and free, male and female (Gal 3:28), yet in spite of this formidable diversity the church is destined to display a unique oneness. While this unity is often difficult to detect in everyday life, it is still at the heart of God's design and intention. In this regard it is important to remember that reconciliation with God has implications for relationships with others, both within the body of Christ and beyond.

---

9. Colin Kruse, *John: An Introduction and Commentary*, Tyndale New Testament Commentaries 4 (Nottingham: IVP Books, 2008; Olive Tree Bible Software), on v. 35.

10. Gary M. Burge, *John*, NIV Application Commentary (Grand Rapids, MI: Zondervan, 2000), on v. 35.

11. "It is not alone the law for a new time, but a law for a new life." George R. Beasley-Murray, *John*, Word Biblical Commentary 36, commentary on Jn. 13:34–35 (Nashville, TN: Thomas Nelson, 1999; Olive Tree Bible Software).

12. See the discussion on pp. 73–75.

The Church as a Unified Body of Believers

Craig Van Gelder's *Essence of the Church* highlights the church as a community of people who are reconciled both with God and with one another.[13] Christ has brought people together in one body not merely to worship God and enjoy the privilege of communion with him. Rather, they are called into community, as they now belong together within one family. It is simply incomprehensible for Christians to remain separated from fellow believers, merely on the grounds of ethnic or clan affiliation, social class, educational background, or any other identity marker. Allowing any such distinctions to split Christians into separate congregations or communities is incompatible with the reconciling power of Christ, whose purpose it was "to create in himself one new humanity out of the two [Jews and Gentiles], thus making peace, and in one body to reconcile both of them to God through the cross, by which he put to death their hostility" (Eph 2:15–16). Throughout the New Testament, and particularly in the Pauline epistles, believers are exhorted to strive for unity and mutual love as the natural outgrowth of the fact that "there is one body and one Spirit, just as you were called to one hope when you were called; one Lord, one faith, one baptism; one God and Father of all, who is over all and through all and in all" (Eph 4:4–6).

The Church as a Called Community

Not only is the church a unified body, but it is also a community with a specific calling. When the apostle Peter addresses his readers as "a chosen people, a royal priesthood, a holy nation, God's special possession" (1 Pet 2:9), he accentuates in the same verse the fact that they were "called . . . out of darkness." Thus, the church is a called-out community, separated from darkness, from evil, and from the world. As the people of Israel were led out of Egypt, so the followers of Christ are called to move out of darkness and into God's presence, toward "his eternal glory in Christ" (1 Pet 5:10). However, Peter makes it clear in his epistles that following Christ entails hardship. Thus, it is also a call to suffering, for "to this you were called, because Christ suffered for you, leaving you an example, that you should follow in his steps" (1 Pet 2:21).[14] This call to suffering is linked with obedience to Christ, a theme developed by Paul in his exhortations to the Romans and to Timothy, whom he also called to live a life of holiness (Rom 1:5–7; 1 Tim 6:12; 2 Tim 1:9) – something which is also stressed by Peter. Third, the church as a community is not only called out

---

13. Van Gelder, *Essence of the Church*, 108.

14. Cf. also 1 Pet 3:9.

of darkness and into fellowship with Christ, but it is also called to be church together. Like Peter, the apostle Paul addresses the members of the church in Corinth as "those sanctified in Christ Jesus and *called to be his holy people, together with all* those everywhere who call on the name of our Lord Jesus Christ" (1 Cor 1:2, italics added). Likewise, in the Epistle to the Ephesians, Paul exhorts his readers to maintain unity and peace, with an appeal to the fact that they form "one body and one Spirit, just as you were *called to one hope when you were called*" (Eph 4:4, italics added). Similarly, in Colossians 3:15 he admonishes the Colossians to "let the peace of Christ rule in your hearts, since as members of one body you were called to peace." The concept of the church as community together is essential if the church is to function as a missional community. The church does not exist in and for itself, but is called both out of and into the world. As church members live and serve together, they are equipped to impact the society around them.[15]

As a called community the church today has an obligation to live out its calling in the particular context in which it finds itself. This may have been much simpler and more straightforward in an era when the whole community revolved around the church and where government and culture were largely aligned with a Christian worldview and values. These conditions, however, are hard to find in our postmodern and predominantly post- or non-Christian world. Consequently, Christians face the challenge of demonstrating their faith in an indifferent, or even antagonistic, environment. Closing themselves off from the outside world is not an option for those who take the clear commands of Scripture to heart. This requires the courage to explore the intersection between faith and societal values. If reconciliation has any significance beyond the relationship between an individual believer and God, it must have implications both within the Christian community and in society at large. Christians have a responsibility as agents of reconciliation, as peacemakers, in situations characterized by brokenness and suffering.[16]

---

15. J. R. Woodward, *Creating a Missional Culture: Equipping the Church for the Sake of the World* (Downers Grove, IL: InterVarsity Press, 2013), 75. Woodward points out the missional hermeneutic of Ephesians 4, where "leaders learn to lead from the margins as priests ministering to fellow priests, with Christ drawing all of us toward himself at the center."

16. Rowan, "Proclaiming the Peacemaker," 49. "In the midst of the brokenness and suffering of the world, the church exists as a community of reconciliation, pointing back to the unique reconciling work of God in Christ on the cross, and pointing forward, by its work and witness, to the ultimate reconciliation of 'all things.'"

The Church as a Multiethnic Mosaic

Having established the essential unity and interconnectedness of the church, it is necessary to underline the organic diversity within the body of Christ, both locally and worldwide. The intrinsic nature of and the need for unity within the church is repeatedly emphasized in Scripture, particularly in the New Testament epistles.[17] Diversity within the Christian community is not incompatible with this fundamental unity, as both are rooted in the unity of the Trinity.[18] Therefore, diversity should not be equated with disunity, or seen as an expression of brokenness. Van Gelder expresses this fittingly: "Rather than contrasting the church's oneness with its brokenness, it is more helpful to see its unity in conjunction with its diversity. That is, the church, while existing as one, also must exist as many."[19] There is thus no inconsistency between the church's unity and its diversity, just as there is no incongruity between the oneness of God and his existence in three persons. Diversity expresses as much of the church's essence as does its oneness. This is emphasized by Paul when he says that God's intent is that "through the church, the manifold wisdom of God should be made known to the rulers and authorities in the heavenly realms" (Eph 3:10).[20]

Such diversity may be expressed in a number of ways, the most important of which are socioeconomic, educational, and ethnic identity. In this context the focus will be primarily on ethnic diversity in the church. The literature review showed that the early church made significant efforts to overcome social, racial, and other biases.[21] While the early church initially consisted mainly of Jewish-background believers, they came from a wide variety of cultural and linguistic contexts. When tensions arose between them, the apostles did not attempt to resolve the conflict by separating them into homogeneous units, but instead appointed leaders from a variety of ethnic groups (Acts 6:1–6). Social and class distinctions were abolished by exhorting masters to fellowship together with slaves as fellow believers in Christ (1 Cor 7:17–24; Phlm 8–16). James commands rich and poor to fellowship together in unity, rather than

---

17. Cf. Rom 12:4–5; 1 Cor 12:12–14; Eph 2:16; 3:6; 4:4, 25; Col 3:15; and others.

18. Cf. Van Gelder, *Essence of the Church*, 122.

19. Van Gelder, 121.

20. This is accentuated by Aubrey Sequeira in "Re-thinking Homogeneity: The Biblical Case for Multi-Ethnic Churches," in *Multi-Ethnic Churches*, ed. Jonathan Leeman, 9Marks Journal IX (Washington DC: 9Marks, 25 Sep. 2015), 30. He argues that "establishing multi-ethnic churches is not only more faithful to Scripture, but . . . multi-ethnic churches more fully display the glorious gospel of Jesus Christ."

21. Cf. the development of the early church in Acts, pp. 58–59.

remain separate along socioeconomic lines (Jas 2:1–9). Aubrey Sequeira argues that "while homogeneity in churches simply *reinforces the status quo of society*, the biblical evidence shows us that the *gospel broke down and cut across ethnic, social, economic, and cultural barriers in ways never before seen in history.*"[22] Jesus and the apostles never encouraged ethnocentrism, but rather called Christians to embrace one another in spite of their differences. Sequeira takes a stand against the Church Growth theory of Donald McGavran, which promotes the "homogeneous unit principle" according to which the gospel spreads most rapidly and easily along the lines of homogeneous units in order to grow the church. Sequeira contends that "while the 'homogeneous unit principle' emphasizes seeking to win people by not offending their ethnocentric sensibilities, Jesus's approach is radically different – Christ lays the axe to the root of ethnic pride."[23] The accounts in the book of Acts demonstrate that churches were not established or separated along ethnic, sociocultural, or class lines. While it may be true that in practice people prefer not to have to cross racial, linguistic, or class barriers when they become Christians, this does not establish a normative biblical pattern. The truth is that reconciliation to God also brings a person into a community "where people find their identity in Jesus Christ rather than in their race, culture, social class, or sex, and are consequently reconciled to one another."[24]

It should be acknowledged, however, that diversity is not the same as reconciliation, and the goal of reconciliation is not simply diversity. As Jarvis Williams helpfully points out, "an assembly of the United Nations is multiethnic and diverse, as is the army, or the local public high school, or so many other

---

22. Sequeira, "Re-thinking Homogeneity," 31–32 (italics original). Sequeira further contends: "Throughout the NT we see an attack on ethnocentrism, and consequently, a mandate for believers from differing ethnic backgrounds to accept each other lovingly and to live together in harmony in local churches."

23. Sequeira, 33. Against Donald McGavran's insistence that the Jew-Gentile separation was not an ethnic issue, Sequeira asserts that "though there are some points of discontinuity between the Jew-Gentile divide and modern ethno-cultural divides, there are enough points of continuity to warrant the parallel. Furthermore, the New Testament does extend the call to unity beyond 'Jew' and 'Gentile' to include categories like 'Barbarian' and 'Scythian,' which are ethnolinguistic categories (Col 3:11). In the New Testament, unity in Christ trumps all other issues of identity, and the call to embrace the 'other' encompasses all categories of 'otherness,' and takes shape in the form of life together in the local church" (35, footnote).

24. Sequeira, 34. In a footnote he quotes René Padilla, *Unity of the Church*, 25: "The extension of the gospel to the Gentiles was such a difficult step for the Jerusalem church that it took place only with the aid of visions and commands ([Acts] 8:26; 10:1–16) or under the pressure of persecution (8:1–3; 11:19–20)." Sequeira, 35.

groups. Yet such settings hardly enjoy the racial reconciliation of the gospel."[25] At the same time, the issue is not always a matter of a majority culture seeking to dominate other (minority) cultures. Often ethnic minority communities choose to meet separately in an effort to preserve and sustain their cultural identity. Patrick Cho, writing about the challenge for Asian churches in North America to become more multiethnic, comments that "most cultures do not want a melting pot as much as an acknowledgement of cultural identity. To use a culinary analogy, perhaps *a truly multiethnic church would look less like a monochrome chowder and more like a varicolored minestrone.*"[26] This observation is particularly helpful as it emphasizes that unity in diversity does not necessarily lead to or require uniformity. The image of a colorful cauldron of minestrone soup conveys a helpful message. Other helpful metaphors might be a multicolored tapestry, a multifaceted diamond, or a colorful multiethnic. Each of these pictures is an image of diversity in harmonious unity. The overall unity does not subsume the identity of its individual components, but rather its composite nature enhances the overall beauty and contributes to its harmony.

Becoming a Missional Church in Myanmar

As indicated in chapter 2, the church in Myanmar has experienced a high level of fragmentation along ethnic as well as theological dividing lines.[27] Viewed from a practical as well as a historical perspective, this development is understandable. This is particularly true where these ethnic divisions are reinforced by language barriers, which make communication with other ethnic groups more difficult.

The Obstacle of Ethnicity-Based Denominationalism

In some minority areas the older population is generally not comfortable in the national language, Burmese.[28] In addition, some minorities, such as the

---

25. Jarvis J. Williams, "Racial Reconciliation, the Gospel, and the Church," in Leeman, *Multi-Ethnic Churches*, 9.

26. Patrick Cho, "Helping Asian Churches Become Multi-Ethnic," in Leeman, *Multi-Ethnic Churches*, 67 (italics added).

27. See "Denominational Division an Obstacle for Witness," pp. 24–25.

28. Or Myanmar language, as it is now more commonly referred to. Younger people are mostly educated in Myanmar language, although they are often at a disadvantage in the education system because they have deficiencies in that area. For this reason the introduction of bilingual or mother-tongue education has recently been advocated; see Yen Saning, "Mother-

Chin, consist of multiple subgroups, each speaking separate languages, and thus they are not even able to communicate with one another unless they use a common language, such as Burmese or English. This has had a twofold effect: some groups have opted to use Burmese, thereby strengthening interethnic connection and belonging, while at the same time being more accessible to other ethnic groups. Others have chosen to worship in their particular ethnic language, whether due to a dislike of the national language or out of a desire to maintain their ethnic identity.[29] Given the pressures and discrimination many ethnic minorities have encountered from the Burman majority, this desire to preserve and cultivate their own ethnic identity is to be expected.[30] Samuel Ngun Ling, discussing the barriers experienced by Christians in Myanmar, offers the following observations:

> Freedom of religion in Myanmar is propagandized only with . . . lip service and never in practice so that strict rules are being set and permissions are often required for Christian meetings, conferences, evangelistic campaign[s], mission fields, church buildings, Christian publications, and many others. . . . Among the restrictions that [have] hindered Christians and other non-Buddhist minorities for years [from fully enjoying] their rights and freedom of faith and expression are such things as refusing to give permission [for] setting up the Christian churches or institutional buildings, non-issuance of passports for the Christian pastors, . . . censorship of . . . Christian literary works, and limited freedom of preaching and propagation of the Christian gospel among the Burman Buddhists.[31]

It is not surprising, therefore, if Christians are reluctant to open their doors (and hearts) to this dominant Buddhist majority, and instead opt for

---

Tongue Instruction Pushed for Burma's Schools," The Irrawaddy, 4 February 2014, https://www.irrawaddy.com/news/burma/mother-tongue-instruction-pushed-burmas-schools.html.

29. Thus there are Chin churches identifying as Asho, Falam, Lai, Lautu, Mizo, or Zomi. Karen churches are usually divided into Pwo Karen and Sgaw Karen, and Methodists have Telugu and Tamil churches (Salay Hta Oke, Yangon Directory).

30. "A number of ethnic peoples especially from among the religiously divided ethnic groups such as the Karen, the Shan, the Mon and the Rakhine are today discovered . . . fully assimilated into the Buddhist religion and culture, using the Burman Buddhist names, Burman language and Burman Buddhist culture at the cost of risking their [existing] ethnic language, religion and culture. This assimilation process historically known as 'Burmanization' was and still is threatening the cultural values and identities of the ethnic minorities in Myanmar." Ngun Ling, "Ethnicity, Religion and Theology in Asia," 3.

31. Ngun Ling, Christianity through Our Neighbors' Eyes, 159–60.

the safety and familiarity of their own culture and community.[32] However, while the demarcation along ethnic and language lines is understandable, at least in minority areas where the population consists largely of a single ethnic group, it is not particularly helpful for a church wanting to be missional. Using a minority language almost certainly precludes people from other ethnicities from joining, or at least from feeling welcome. This is especially relevant in multicultural urban settings, such as Yangon and other major cities that form a melting pot of cultures and ethnicities.

The Challenge of the Clergy-Laity Division

As observed previously, the transition toward a division between clergy and laity in the church was precipitated more by historical than theological causes.[33] The Edict of Milan (AD 313), guaranteeing religious toleration, and the Edict of Thessalonica (AD 380), which established Christianity as the sole recognized religion of the Roman Empire, served to reinforce and expand the role and position of bishops and members of the clergy in the church (and in society).[34] While the Reformation sought to emphasize the priesthood of all believers, it was less successful in removing the barrier between clergy and laity in the church.[35]

The role of pastors, evangelists, and other ordained clergy is prominent in churches throughout Myanmar. Their names are clearly displayed on noticeboards, bulletins, and websites, which often include their academic credentials and titles. Religious ceremonies (baptism, communion, commissioning) and preaching are usually reserved for those who have been properly trained and ordained. Pastoral visits are normally expected to be carried out by the pastor, rather than an ordinary church member or even an elder. Pastors and Bible teachers are highly respected within the Christian community, and young people from Christian families are often encouraged to go to Bible college and enter Christian ministry.[36] This stems in part from

---

32. While the Burman majority may be in the best position to initiate ethnic reconciliation (cf. Walton, "Wages of Burman-Ness," 12–14), there is a missional imperative on the Christian community to act as "agents of reconciliation," in spite of the suffering and marginalization they have suffered.

33. See the discussion on p. 39.

34. Easley and Morgan, *Community of Jesus*, loc. 3819, Kindle.

35. Van Gelder, *Essence of the Church*, 58.

36. VL, interview with the author on Christian witness in Buddhist Myanmar, 24 November 2014; Ganzevoort, "Myanmar Experiences," 10.

the fact that university education in Myanmar in recent decades has not been of a high standard and university degrees have offered few tangible benefits after graduation. For decades, even an unaccredited Bible degree has provided opportunities for young people from a poor background in a country with few other prospects.[37] The more significant motive, however, would seem to be the belief that serving in Christian ministry is somehow a higher calling than working in a secular profession. A person who commits his or her life to such ministry is often considered more spiritual than an ordinary Christian.[38]

Some Christian leaders from Myanmar recognize the problem of this "clergy-laity bifurcation," as Morris Remlal Liana calls it.[39] They point out that pastors in Myanmar find it difficult to share their ministry with laypeople. The reason given is that if pastors get too close to the laypeople, the pastors will be taken advantage of. This often results in a distance between clergy and laity.[40] Liana, serving with the Wesleyan Church of Myanmar, observes that, first, a

> centuries-long history of authoritarian leadership and deference to elders and leaders in Myanmar surfaces in the Church in leadership attitudes and behaviors that do not nurture the Church. Second, and closely related to this first problem, church leaders prove unwilling and/or unable to share ministry with laypersons. In many of the Churches, the lone doers are clergy; the laity has become spectators, watching from the pews. Some pastors see their inability to do all the work in the Church by themselves, but lack leadership skills to engage their congregations in ministry. Others do not seem to grasp the need or options for developing leadership and partners in ministry among the laypeople.[41]

This sentiment is echoed by Karen Baptist Saw Gler Taw, who comments that "the professional elite minority 'jealously holds the fort' . . . leading to discrimination and failure to recognize the Kayin laity."[42] Exploring the

---

37. JMB, interview with the author on Christian witness in Buddhist Myanmar, 26 November 2014; Ngun Ling, *Christianity through Our Neighbors' Eyes*, 78.

38. GCZ, interview with the author on Christian witness in Buddhist Myanmar.

39. Morris Remlal Liana, "Developing Servant Leadership in the Wesleyan Church of Myanmar" (DMin diss., Asbury Theological Seminary, 2004), 45–46.

40. Cin Do Kham, "Historical Values and Modes of Leadership in Myanmar: Assessment of Roots of Values among Christian Leaders in Yangon" (PhD diss., Trinity International University, 1998), 122–23; Liana, "Developing Servant Leadership," 14–15.

41. Liana, 77–78.

42. Saw Gler Taw, "Factors Affecting the Growth of the Kayin Baptist Church with a View toward Facilitating Renewal" (DMiss diss., Fuller Theological Seminary, 1996), 163–64.

possible reasons for such a failure to engage the lay portion of the Christian community, Cin Do Kham suggests that Christian leaders may be unwittingly following Buddhist culture by maintaining a distance between clergy and laity. He points out that, just like Buddhist monks who are considered to be above common people and as such receive respect, Christian leaders become isolated. In Myanmar culture, people must obey their leaders in everything, and thus Christian leaders usually keep a distance from laypeople.[43]

In a blog article on the topic "Laypeople and the Mission of God," Ed Stetzer, dean of the School of Mission, Ministry, and Leadership at Wheaton College, and Executive Director of the Wheaton College Billy Graham Center, notes:

> Every church must have a strategy and a process to equip people for ministry and mission. Thus, they create an environment where people are empowered and enabled to do ministry. . . . There is a role for leadership, but we cannot miss the reality that, in most churches, there are many more passive spectators than there are active participants in the mission of God.[44]

A missional church will naturally involve, equip, and enable its members to engage in ministry. If, on the other hand, church leaders neglect to involve their members or even hinder their participation, the church will lose its missional focus and the members are at risk of becoming passive bystanders.

Although the New Testament clearly states that all God's people are priests (1 Pet 2:9) and ministers (1 Pet 4:10), the reality is that people often expect someone to go to God *for* them and do the ministry *for* them. However, if God appoints leaders "to equip the saints for the work of ministry, for building up the body of Christ" (Eph 4:12 ESV), there is no need to perpetuate this system. Perhaps pastors secretly derive their identity from doing the ministry rather than from training and equipping God's people for ministry. Or, they may be afraid that if they train their congregation to do the ministry, the pastor will not be needed anymore. However, it is essential that pastors equip God's people for ministry, not "be the shopkeeper of the religious store providing religious rituals to ceremonialize devotion," as Stetzer articulates it.[45]

---

43. Cin Do Kham, "Historical Values," 122.

44. Ed Stetzer, "Laypeople and the Mission of God: Part 2 – Reclaiming the Priesthood of All Believers," https://www.visionroom.com/laypeople-and-the-mission-of-god-part-2/, accessed 7 April 2022.

45. Stetzer, "Laypeople and the Mission of God."

The Need for Contextualization

In the eyes of the Buddhist majority in Myanmar, Christianity is a foreign religion, as discussed in chapter 2.[46] Since the reign of King Anawratha (AD 1044–1077), Burman culture and values have been deeply influenced by Theravada Buddhism, shaping their thoughts, ideas, morality, and philosophy.[47] When Western Protestant missionaries arrived in the nineteenth century, starting with the American Baptists, they were seen as part of the Western military's economic and political occupation of Burma.[48] Thus far the Christian church in Myanmar has not been able to shed its Western identity, which remains visible in the lifestyle of Burmese Christians, their worship style, and their evangelistic messages and methodologies.[49]

While the need for contextualization is generally acknowledged by missiologists across the theological spectrum, the concept remains controversial and suspect among some evangelicals.[50] It is therefore perhaps not surprising to encounter an abundance of understandings of contextualization. Jackson Wu, author of *One Gospel for All Nations*, lists no fewer than thirteen different definitions and offers the following as his own contribution: "Contextualization is the interpretation, communication, and application of the biblical text in view of a cultural context."[51] Given the confusion around the term, it is perhaps helpful to distinguish contextualization from syncretism. Michael Poon, in *Christian Movements in Southeast Asia*, suggests that

> contextualization is sensitive to the issues, concerns and thought forms of the context. It tries to address these issues and concerns in a way consistent with the larger Christian tradition. When borrowing terms and ideas from the context, these are always reinterpreted in accordance with biblical theology. Syncretism, on

---

46. See pp. 20–21.

47. Lindsay Jones, *Encyclopedia of Religion*, vol. 9, 2nd ed. (Farmington Hills, MI: Thomson-Gale, 2005), 6427; Liana, "Developing Servant Leadership," 9.

48. Kam, "Christian Mission to Buddhists in Myanmar," 214.

49. These are the areas proposed as in need of contextualization by Tint Lwin in "Contextualization of the Gospel: An Effective Strategy for the Evangelization of the Theravada Buddhists in Myanmar" (PhD diss., Southern Baptist Theological Seminary, 1997), 174.

50. Cf. David J. Hesselgrave, ed., *Missionshift: Global Mission Issues in the Third Millennium* (Nashville, TN: Broadman & Holman, 2010), 3: "Contextualization is not the only thing going on in Evangelical missions today, but it is surely the most controversial."

51. Jackson Wu, "How Do Evangelicals Define 'Contextualization'?," Jackson Wu, 24 May 2013, accessed 18 July 2015, http://jacksonwu.org/2013/05/24/how-do-evangelicasl-define-contextualization/; Jackson Wu, *One Gospel for All Nations* (Pasadena, CA: William Carey Library, 2015).

the other hand, appropriates substantial elements from the context to bring together gospel and context. The end result is that instead of the gospel challenging culture, it becomes a part of culture.[52]

Although few publications on the need for contextualization are available in Myanmar, some scholars have written theses or dissertations on this topic.[53] Some authors, like C. Duh Kam, focus on contextualization of theological terms, forms of discipleship similar to the monkhood, and religious festivals, as well as more outward issues, such as church architecture.[54] Khai Chin Khua addresses the need for appropriate forms of worship and music, the use of redemptive analogies and symbols, and prophetic movements.[55] Similarly, Tint Lwin proposes several areas for consideration: the lifestyle of Burmese Christians (dress, attitude toward traditional legends, music, dance, and poetry), Christian worship (church architecture and music), evangelistic methodologies (cultural sensitivity and respect, and conversion as a process), and the content of the Christian message (Christian response to Buddhist concepts such as *Annica, Dukkha, Anatta, Karma, Samsara,* and *Nirvana*; and the challenge of God as Creator).[56]

Baptist theologian Saw Say Khu, who focused his dissertation on the need for contextual models of church growth in Myanmar, suggests an emphasis on Christian attitude, lifestyle, and message. He advocates a strategy based around discipleship, using home cell groups that promote both quantitative and qualitative growth.[57] Furthermore, he contends for the integration of

---

52. Michael Nai-Chiu Poon, *Christian Movements in Southeast Asia: A Theological Exploration*, CSCA Christianity in Southeast Asia (Singapore: Genesis Books, 2010), 5.

53. Kam, "Christian Mission to Buddhists in Myanmar"; Tint Lwin, "Contextualization of the Gospel"; Khai Chin Khua, "Dynamics of Renewal: A Historical Movement among the Zomi (Chin) in Myanmar" (PhD diss., Fuller Theological Seminary, 1999); Pum Za Thang Tombing, "Training Zomi Christian Leaders for Missions to Hindus and Buddhists" (DMin diss., Oral Roberts University, 2002); Van Ram Oke, "Missioners as Contextualizers: The Theology and Practice of Contextualization in the Ministry of Bread of Life to the Bama Community of New Dagon City" (DMin diss., Asia Graduate School of Theology, 2007); Saw Say Khu, "Contextual Models for Church Growth in Myanmar" (DMin diss., Union Theological Seminary Philippines & Myanmar Institute of Theology, 2007); Nang Gin Khan, "Zomi Christianity and Cultural Transformation" (PhD diss., Fuller Theological Seminary, 2010); Peter Thein Nyunt, *Missions amidst Pagodas: Contextual Communication of the Gospel in Burmese Buddhist Context* (Yangon: Myint Offset, 2012).

54. Kam, "Christian Mission to Buddhists in Myanmar," 220–46.

55. Khai Chin Khua, "Dynamics of Renewal," 343–53.

56. Tint Lwin, "Contextualization of the Gospel," 174–257. Tint Lwin offers many helpful suggestions, some of which will be explored later.

57. Saw Say Khu, "Contextual Models for Church Growth in Myanmar," 64–81.

evangelism with social service. He points out that under colonial rule the missionaries and the church were strongly engaged in social programs, but after the nationalization of mission schools and hospitals, Christianity lost its role in social development for several decades. Both as a demonstration of Christian love and as a preparation for preaching the gospel message, social service has crucial significance.[58]

The Importance of Outward-Focused Discipleship

As indicated above, Saw Say Khu considers discipleship an important element for church growth in Myanmar. In fact, he asserts that lack of assurance of salvation is one of the main reasons why Myanmar Christians are not active in evangelism.[59] Certainly a basic conviction regarding one's faith is indispensable for meaningful spiritual dialogue. Missional churches develop from an integral approach to spiritual formation that seeks to nurture followers of Christ into mature believers who live out their faith in dependence on God and for his glory.[60] The discipleship process needs to be rooted in biblical values, but it also needs to engage with the worldview and cultural values of the society in which people live.[61] The Indian intellectual and philosopher Vishal Mangalwadi has called for a social transformation driven by the church and based on biblical,

---

58. Saw Say Khu, 89.

59. Saw Say Khu, "Assurance of Salvation," *Myanmar Pastor* (blog), 3 September 2007, accessed 8 April 2018, http://myanmarpastor.blogspot.com/2007/09/assurance-of-salvation.html.

60. This is the approach offered by Dallas Willard in *The Divine Conspiracy: Rediscovering Our Hidden Life in God* (San Francisco: HarperCollins, 1998).

61. The following example is from a term paper for the course "Developing Missional Churches in Asian Contexts": Floyd McClung's ministry in Amsterdam's red light district was sometimes met with angry or hateful responses from the locals involved in the sex trade. McClung learned to respond not with the same attitude of anger or hate, but instead with love and kindness, thereby breaking through the resistance put up by their defenses: "All of us must learn to live out our ordinary, everyday lives in the power of the Spirit. It means responding to people in the opposite spirit to that which we see around us – showing purity where there is immorality, peace instead of violence, forgiveness rather than bitterness, and generosity in place of greed and selfishness." When Christians in Myanmar encounter an attitude of ethnic or religious pride, how would it be if these followers of Jesus responded with sincere meekness? And what if – when people are bent on trying to control their destiny – Christians show that their trust is in God alone? Finally, rather than pursuing wealth or a more comfortable life, Christians could make serving others their priority. By turning society's values on their head, Christ's disciples will at the same time engage and challenge these norms. Rather than becoming ingrown and self-focused, the church will transform not only individuals, but society as a whole. Arend Van Dorp, "Developing Missional Churches in the Myanmar Context" (TM751 term paper, Fuller Theological Seminary, 2015), 35.

spiritual values. He contends that it was Christianity that brought the West to greatness, while much of Africa, Asia, and the Middle East remained in poverty, injustice, and hopelessness.[62] As Myanmar has been ravaged by decades of oppression, it faces a multitude of social, political, religious, and educational issues. At this critical time in history, the church may have to make a choice either to be inward-focused, seeking to safeguard its position and avoid drawing attention to itself, or to rise up to the challenge and engage with a clear biblical vision for transformation of the nation, which for decades has been plagued by ethnic and religious strife.

Working toward Reconciliation and Diversity

This outward-focused discipleship will be needed for the church to fulfill its calling to be a light to the nations, a royal priesthood representing Christ and demonstrating the transforming power of reconciliation. In 2 Corinthians 5 Paul makes it abundantly clear that our reconciliation with God makes believers into agents of reconciliation, as God "reconciled us to himself through Christ and gave us the ministry of reconciliation" (5:18).[63] Obviously, such a ministry cannot be fulfilled unless this reconciliation extends to one another. Paul made that clear when he said to the Corinthians regarding a repentant brother that they "ought to forgive and comfort him, so that he will not be overwhelmed by excessive sorrow."[64]

Reconciliation with God and with One Another

Reconciliation has only recently been recognized as a significant missiological theme.[65] However, starting with Miroslav Volf in 1997, and continuing during the last two decades, the topic has received significant attention at theological conferences.[66] Volf argues that in order for Christian communities to become

---

62. Vishal Mangalwadi, *Truth and Transformation: A Manifesto for Ailing Nations* (Seattle: YWAM, 2009), 40–42.

63. Miroslav Volf writes, "Though reconciliation of human beings to God has priority, reconciliation between human beings is intrinsic to their reconciliation to God." Miroslav Volf, "The Social Meaning of Reconciliation," *Occasional Papers on Religion in Eastern Europe* 18, no. 3 (1998): 7, accessed 21 October 2017, http://digitalcommons.georgefox.edu/ree/vol18/iss3/3.

64. 2 Cor 2:7. Also Eph 4:32 and Col 3:13, where Paul exhorts believers to "forgiv[e] each other, just as in Christ God forgave you."

65. David Bosch treats reconciliation only in passing (Bosch, *Transforming Mission*, 394).

66. For a helpful overview of these developments, see Rowan, "Proclaiming the Peacemaker," 54.

peacemakers and reconcilers in situations of ethnic conflict, they need not only to understand the biblical message of reconciliation, but also, and more importantly, to comprehend "the inherent social meaning of reconciliation."[67] Too often, according to Volf, reconciliation has been either reduced to the restoration of an individual relationship with God, or replaced by the pursuit of social justice and liberation. He consequently argues for an understanding of reconciliation with both vertical and horizontal dimensions. This becomes evident from his conviction that "though grace is unthinkable without justice, justice is subordinate to grace," and "though reconciliation of human beings to God has priority, reconciliation between human beings is intrinsic to their reconciliation to God."[68]

While forgiveness and reconciliation on the individual level are often difficult enough, these issues become even more challenging on a group level. Myanmar society, with its deep-rooted and entrenched divisions, presents a daunting setting for the church to be a reconciled and reconciling community. A major contributor to this problem is the fact that identity (both individual and communal) is usually bound up with ethnicity.[69] Volf (quoting Jacob Neusner) challenges Christians to consider that "the ultimate allegiance of those whose father is Abraham can be only to the God of 'all families of the earth,' not to any particular country, culture, or family with their local deities."[70] Elaborating on how God's election of one man, Abraham, can serve as an instrument of blessing for all nations (peoples), Volf explains the connection between universality and particularity:

> The oneness of God requires God's universality; God's universality entails human equality; human equality implies equal access by all to the blessings of the one God; equal access is incompatible with ascription of religious significance to genealogy; Christ, the seed of Abraham, is both the fulfillment of the genealogical promise to Abraham and the end of genealogy as a privileged locus of access to God; faith in Christ replaces birth into a people. As a consequence, all people can have access to the one God of

---

67. Volf, "Social Meaning of Reconciliation," 12.

68. Volf, 7.

69. Miroslav Volf, *Exclusion and Embrace: A Theological Exploration of Identity, Otherness, and Reconciliation* (Nashville, TN: Abingdon Press, 2010), 37. Volf, quoting Ralph Premdas, comments: "Along with their parishioners the clergy are often 'trapped within the claims of their own ethnic or cultural community' and thus serve as 'legitimators of ethnic conflict,' their genuine desire to take seriously the Gospel call to the ministry of reconciliation notwithstanding."

70. Volf, *Exclusion and Embrace*, 39.

Abraham and Sarah on equal terms, none by right and all by grace.[71]

Thus, through faith in Christ, all of humanity is welcomed into God's family. Christians need to avoid creating a new, separate culture by which they would isolate themselves from their own. Instead, while stepping with one foot outside their culture, they should remain with the other foot within it. Although separate and different from others, they still belong. These are the paradoxes of the Christian church: united yet diverse, separate though still belonging, fostering community without exclusion.

However, inclusion is not the end point. In order to move from inclusion to embrace, another step is needed: forgiveness. In a fractured and divided society like Myanmar this is a sensitive topic. The reality is that almost all people consider themselves victims in one way or another. Minorities have experienced violence and harassment perpetrated by the majority Bamar, while many Bamar themselves would argue that they, too, have been victims of army and police brutality, and even the military will contend that they have been obliged to use force because of provocations by the ethnic armed groups.[72] Almost no group is prepared to acknowledge responsibility for their role in the continuing conflicts in the country.[73] Consequently, the vicious cycle of violence, suffering, and hatred continues, making a resolution to the conflict more difficult to achieve. Volf's portrayal of the situation is as poignant as it is tragic: "If perpetrators were repentant, forgiveness would come more easily. But too often they are not. And so, both victim and perpetrator are imprisoned in the automatism of mutual exclusion, unable to forgive or repent and united in a perverse communion of hate."[74] In addition, even if there is a recognition of responsibility and culpability, the harm and suffering can never be undone.

---

71. Volf, 45.

72. Walton, "Wages of Burman-Ness," 16.

73. Walton, 20.

74. Volf, *Exclusion and Embrace*, 120. Jelle van Essen, in his study of the post–Cold War interethnic conflict in the former Yugoslavia, observes that "in most large-scale societal conflicts both antagonistic groups are simultaneously victims and aggressors. Even though both parties are to blame for violent acts, apologies rarely occur for several reasons: First, both parties perceive themselves primarily as victims and not as aggressors. Also, both conflicting groups expect an apology, instead of having to apologize themselves. Third, perpetrators seldom think that they did something wrong during the conflict. They see their abuses as righteous behavior for their country or ethnic group." Jelle P. van Essen, "Recognizing Reconciliation: The Role of Culture on Post World War II and Post-Cold War Reconciliatory Processes and Acts of Apology" (MA diss., Erasmus University, 2014), 18.

As Volf says, "our actions are irreversible."[75] The only way out is through forgiveness, because "unless people manage to forsake their determination to 'get even,' there can be no new beginning, no transformation of relationships. Everyone will remain imprisoned in a particular history or mythology, recycling old crimes and hatreds."[76] Volf's point is not that forgiveness will necessarily bring suffering to an end – in fact forgiveness may be considered in itself a form of suffering – but that it allows the one who forgives to move beyond the wrongdoing and to focus on the future, rather than continue to dwell on the past.

Robert Schreiter, in a lecture on a theology of reconciliation, points out that reconciliation is first and foremost the work of God. However, when examining reconciliation between people, he stresses that God's reconciling work begins with the victim. God's healing work in the victim sometimes makes it possible for the victim to forgive the wrongdoer even before repentance takes place.[77] This may result in a transformation of both the victim and the wrongdoer. Suffering, although not good in and of itself, can acquire meaning in the context of Christ's suffering. However, reconciliation will be complete only once God has eradicated all suffering.

Cho Cho Myaing, writing specifically in the context of the situation in Myanmar, concludes that forgiveness is the primary way toward a fundamental transformation of both victim and perpetrator and that it should play a central role in both social and individual transformation.[78] This has profound implications, not only for Christian community, but also for evangelism, as I. Howard Marshall notes:

> Those who make known the gospel and who live as Christians in the world share the reconciling love of the God whose servants they are. They cannot very well preach a gospel of reconciliation to a people with whom they themselves are not prepared to live in peace and love. One cannot shout the gospel across a chasm to

---

75. Volf, *Exclusion and Embrace*, 121.

76. Van Essen, "Recognizing Reconciliation," 18, quoting Hannah Arendt, *The Human Condition* (New York, 1959), 213.

77. Robert J. Schreiter, "Theology of Reconciliation and Peacemaking for Mission," 2003 Lectures for the British and Irish Association of Mission Studies, New College, University of Edinburgh, 23–25 June 2003, accessed 19 June 2017, http://www.ehcounseling.com/materials/_applied_theology_of_reconciliation.pdf. Also, Robert J. Schreiter, "Reconciliation as a Model of Mission," *New Theology Review* 10, no. 2 (1997), 11–12.

78. Cho Cho Myaing, "Forgiveness toward National Reconciliation," 74.

people on the other side so that they may have a relationship with God above but not one with those on this side of the chasm.[79]

This is one of the great challenges for the church in Myanmar, as illustrated in chapter 2.[80] For Christians to overcome their fears and reluctance to extend to those from other ethnicities the grace they themselves have received, they need to embrace the reality of their own reconciliation with God and with one another. Reconciliation is inherently connected with diversity and inclusivity. These themes will be explored in the last section of this chapter.

The Missional Impact of an Inclusive Community

Buddhism has traditionally absorbed a variety of local customs, rituals, and practices, or at least sought to coexist with preexisting religious traditions wherever it has become established.[81] Christianity, on the other hand, has tended to define much clearer boundaries between what is and what is not acceptable in terms of religious practices.[82] To avoid falling into syncretism missionaries have usually drawn clear and strict lines demarcating and restricting inappropriate conduct. While inherently sensible, this has created the notion among Buddhist people that Christians are rigid and intolerant. When a Buddhist learns that "whoever believes in the Son has eternal life, but whoever rejects the Son will not see life, for God's wrath remains on them" (John 3:36), this is seen as prejudiced and narrow-minded. This impression of Christianity as exclusionist and restrictive is bolstered by the perception that church membership is predominantly based on ethnic identity and affiliation.[83]

In order to overcome such perceptions, the church will need to consider its self-understanding in light of the biblical-theological insights established in this chapter. In particular, the unified nature of the church as the body of Christ, its calling as an inclusive community, and its composition as a

79. I. Howard Marshall, *Aspects of the Atonement: Cross and Resurrection in the Reconciling of God and Humanity* (Carlisle: Paternoster, 2007), 134.

80. See "The Church and the Challenge of Reconciliation," pp. 28–34.

81. Roger Bischoff, *Buddhism in Myanmar: A Short History* (Kandi, Sri Lanka: Buddhist Publication Society, 1995), 14; Maung Maung Aye, "Spirit Belief in Burmese Buddhism," 50.

82. U Hla Bu, "The Christian Encounter with Buddhism in Burma," *International Review of Mission* 47, no. 186 (1958): 174; Zam Khat Kham, "Burmese Nationalism," 125.

83. In the context of this book, there is not space to discuss the issue of a contextualized gospel presentation for Myanmar. However, several recent publications have addressed this issue, highlighting the need for a more honor-shame-based approach, e.g. Wu, *One Gospel for All Nations*; Werner Mischke, *The Global Gospel: Achieving Missional Impact in Our Multicultural World* (Scottsdale, AZ: Mission ONE, 2015).

multiethnic mosaic need to receive more attention. Recognizing these aspects of the church as essential will be a vital component in working toward a more missional model for the church in Myanmar.

Part 3

Ministry Practice

5

Steps toward Becoming More Missional

In this chapter we introduce an inclusive model for developing missional churches in Myanmar. This model seeks to promote reconciliation and embrace multiethnic diversity, creating a welcoming environment toward building a transformational community.

Without taking intentional steps and measures, churches may struggle to become more missional. Like any other community and social entity, they have created patterns of behavior and models of operation over time. These have developed into solid traditions establishing a common identity. Moving toward an alternative model of operation will therefore require purposeful planning and deliberate action. In the previous chapter we identified several biblical-theological elements of a missional church model, and we will now develop these into more concrete strategies and plans.

Discipleship Focus: Pursuing Life-Changing Spiritual Formation

While discipleship as a concept and discipleship programs as a practical application have received significant attention in recent years in Myanmar as elsewhere, these efforts have often been focused on individual change and formation.[1] However, as suggested before, discipleship requires a more comprehensive, holistic approach based on a biblical understanding of the church as a welcoming community, a diverse but unified body of followers

---

1. The tendency to focus discipleship efforts on the individual can be seen in the widespread use of discipleship materials often produced in the West and translated into Burmese. These materials tend to limit discipleship to personal spiritual growth through Bible study and the individual's journey of faith.

of Christ. In such a context, discipleship is more than a program to help new believers understand the basic teachings and apply various practices of the Christian life. Not only is it a lifelong process of spiritual growth, it is also a praxis which involves the entire congregation.[2] Moreover, it is not aimed exclusively at the growth of individual believers toward maturity; rather, it involves establishing patterns and practices leading to spiritual transformation of the entire community. Discipleship as a missional church praxis is thus a lifelong process involving the entire congregation and impacting the whole community.[3] Discipleship in a missional perspective thus incorporates the whole of life, the whole church, and the whole of society. The impact of the good news of Jesus Christ in Myanmar will not depend on verbal proclamation only (however essential that is), but also on true, life-changing conduct of Christians within their spheres of influence. The changed lives of church members, both individually and communally demonstrating outward-focused discipleship, will send a powerful message of reconciliation to a society riven by contentious ideologies of ethnic and religious identity.

Inclusive Communities: Embracing Ethnic Diversity in Churches

An environment that accentuates ethnic identity and classifies communities based on their religious affiliation poses a challenge to inclusiveness and ethnic diversity. As Miroslav Volf argues, "the problem of ethnic and cultural conflicts is part of a larger problem of identity and otherness."[4] This inclusive embracing, however, is exactly what the gospel requires and what the church should embody. John Woodward stresses the importance of churches crossing "ethnic, class and age barriers because one of the statements our world needs to see is that there can be unity in diversity when Jesus is king of that community."[5] While the tendency in Myanmar is to emphasize the otherness of divergent ethnic communities, the church as an inclusive community is called to draw people together rather than separate them. Christians must learn, according to one theological student from Myanmar, to

> accept not only the unity of humanity but also the cultural
> diversity that ethnic groups bring to the churches in Myanmar

---

2. Branson and Martínez, *Churches, Cultures and Leadership*, 43.

3. Branson and Martínez, 42. "No one learns from experience. One learns only from experience one reflects upon and articulates."

4. Volf, *Exclusion and Embrace*, 16.

5. Woodward, *Creating a Missional Culture*, 56.

today. One of the tasks of the Church in a given culture is to contribute to the flowering of that culture, as well as to make sure that the salutary sense of ethnic belonging does not turn into ethnic aggressions towards the "stranger who is within the gates" or towards neighboring ethnic groups. It is therefore the responsibility of the Church to work towards genuine community, in which each ethnic group remains faithful to its dynamic and changing identity and yet is enriched by and enriches others.[6]

The penchant toward exclusion does not necessarily stem from a deliberate effort to reject others, but may arise from an unconscious preference for those from their own community and faith tradition. What is needed, therefore, is to realize one's own susceptibility to discrimination, springing from a tendency to reject others who are different from oneself. Once a process of outward-focused discipleship has been initiated, it should foster a new perspective of welcoming and embracing people from an array of ethnic backgrounds.

Mobilization of the Laity: Involving All Members in Ministry

Not only should the church be a welcoming community, whatever one's background or ethnic identity, but it should also engage all members in ministry.[7] This aspect has been discussed in chapter 4 (The Challenge of the Clergy-Laity Division), but it is important to reiterate it here, as there are significant ramifications for the missional impact of the church.[8] Without the active participation of its members, the church in Myanmar may not be able to fulfill its calling as an agent of transformation and reconciliation.

In his book *Creating a Missional Culture*, J. R. Woodward offers a new model for churches from its leadership structure to its mobilization of the laity. He asserts that

> creating a missional culture helps the church live out her calling to be a sign of the kingdom, pointing people to the reality beyond what we can see, a foretaste of the kingdom where we grow to love

---

6. Puia, "Ethnic Diversities and Their Impacts on Today's Churches" (MDiv diss., Myanmar Institute of Theology, 2015), 42.

7. For an examination of the church as a welcoming community, see chapter 4 ("Christ Has Removed the Barriers"), p. 67.

8. Cf. Bosch, *Transforming Mission*, 520; Easley and Morgan, *Community of Jesus*, loc. 3819, Kindle.

one another as Christ loves us, and an instrument in the hands of God to bring more of heaven to earth in concrete ways.[9]

He calls for a new kind of leadership, labeled "polycentric" leadership. His premise is that church leaders should not act as gatekeepers, but equippers. He distinguishes five types of equipping (as seen in table 2) based on Ephesians 4:11–12, linking them to the specific environments they create.[10]

Thus, apostles cultivate a thriving environment, prophets create a liberating environment, evangelists generate a welcoming environment, pastors foster a healing environment, and teachers establish a learning environment. What this model illustrates is the complementarity of polycentric leadership roles in the church and the purpose of each function in creating an enabling environment where church members have opportunities to engage in various aspects of church ministry. Woodward calls on churches and church leaders to cultivate an equipping *ethos*, an environment where leaders act less like multitalented star players and more like coaches and air traffic controllers, enabling and directing others to exercise their God-given abilities.[11] This is vital for churches seeking to involve all members in ministry.

Table 2. Equipping Roles and Missional Environments

Equipper	Thick Practices (Liturgies)	Environments They Cultivate
Apostles (dream awakeners)	Sabbath Making disciples	A thriving environment that calls people to join God in the redemption of all things by developing a strong discipleship ethos
Prophets (heart revealers)	Being present to God (silence, solitude, fasting) Breaking bread	A liberating environment that dares people to embody a holistic gospel, helping people experience liberation from personal and social sins, by forming Spirit-transforming communities

---

9. Woodward, *Creating a Missional Culture*, 29. He also writes, "The church needs a *polycentric approach to leadership*, where the equippers enable their *fellow priests* to live to their sacred potential" (p. 41, italics in original).

10. Woodward, 189. In the context of this book the focus is primarily on the relationship between the role of the equippers and the environments they cultivate.

11. Woodward, 199. Ed Stetzer contrasts this with the traditional role of pastors as being "the shopkeeper of the religious store providing religious rituals to ceremonialize devotion [or] a religious hierarchy to outsource people's religious obligations." Stetzer, "Laypeople and the Mission of God."

Evangelists (storytellers)	Hospitality Sharing God's story	A welcoming environment that invites people to bless their neighbors and be redemptive agents in their vocations
Pastors (soul healers)	Confession Peacemaking	A healing environment in which people learn to embody the ministry of reconciliation and cultivate a life-giving spirituality in God's new family
Teachers (light givers)	Sacred assemblies Future-oriented living	A learning environment where people immerse themselves in God's narrative and engage in praxis and future-oriented living

Contextualized Practices and Communication

As suggested in the previous chapter, there is an urgent need to consider contextualized patterns of Christian life and ministry in Myanmar. Not many published resources are available, either in Burmese or English, although some academic papers can be found in local theological libraries.[12] One of the elements most often mentioned as essential for contextualizing Christianity is the need for a renewed appreciation of Myanmar culture and traditions. Tint Lwin recommends a greater adherence to Myanmar dress code and a deeper appreciation of traditional literature, music, dance, and poetry. He also challenges churches to reconsider Christian worship styles, such as Western music and evangelistic approaches, and to show more respect for indigenous customs and practices. Finally, and perhaps most significantly, he encourages Christians to think through how the Christian gospel message interacts with Buddhist beliefs regarding impermanence, suffering, and selfhood.[13] Van Ram Oke adds several other elements, such as showing appropriate respect rather than a condescending attitude, and serving in practical ways, such as giving attention to physical needs, including healing, as well as deliverance.

---

12. One of the few authors who have published their ideas is Peter Thein Nyunt. His book *Missions amidst Pagodas: Contextual Communication of the Gospel in Burmese Buddhist Context* is available in both Burmese and English. Some examples of unpublished sources are Kam, "Christian Mission to Buddhists in Myanmar"; Saw Say Khu, "Contextual Models for Church Growth in Myanmar"; Tint Lwin, "Contextualization of the Gospel"; and Van Ram Oke, "Missioners as Contextualizers."

13. Tint Lwin, 174–257.

He also suggests considering how the gospel meets felt needs, especially fear and shame.[14]

C. Duh Kam approaches contextualization differently, focusing on the contrast between seemingly similar theological concepts which need clarification in the communication between Buddhists and Christians. Buddhists, influenced by the concept of *karma*, often misunderstand Christ's substitutionary atonement, a key element in Christian soteriology.[15] *Agape* is very different from the Buddhist belief in *metta-karuna*, while the kingdom of God is diametrically opposed to the concept of *samsara-nirvana*.[16] Finally, the relationship between sin and suffering is fundamentally different in Christian and Buddhist thought. Other areas where understandings diverge and misunderstandings can easily arise are the significance of religious buildings (churches versus pagodas) and festivals, and Christian discipleship versus Buddhist monkhood.[17]

Saw Say Khu points out several areas in need of contextualization. First, he notes Christian attitude, especially the need to avoid a sense of superiority or seeing Buddhists as "objects of spiritual conquest."[18] Second, he mentions every Christian's lifestyle, particularly outside the church, in the family and the workplace. Third, he encourages Christians to study Buddhism, in order to be able to share the gospel in a relevant way. Finally, Christians need to explain how Christ sets people free from fear, including fear of the *nats*.[19] In summary, contextualization requires adaptations in the areas of attitude, lifestyle, and accurate, relevant communication of the gospel message.

---

14. Van Ram Oke, "Missioners as Contextualizers," 105–15.

15. Kam, "Christian Mission to Buddhists in Myanmar," 226–28.

16. Kam, 229–33.

17. Kam, 234–45.

18. Saw Say Khu, "Contextual Models for Church Growth in Myanmar," 58.

19. Saw Say Khu, 62.

6

Conclusion

My hope is that this book will inspire the church in Myanmar to expand beyond the confines of its historical boundaries and reach out to the communities around it. To this end we have examined the essential characteristics of the church, such as being a unified body, a called-out community and a multiethnic mosaic. We have looked at how this understanding of the church as one body in Christ (Rom 12), the removal of barriers between believers (Eph 2) and our witness to the world (John 13) may help toward becoming a missional church.

We have also investigated various obstacles to being a missional church in a pluralist society such as Myanmar. These obstacles include the challenges posed by ethnic denominationalism that results in widespread fragmentation among churches, which is so prevalent in Myanmar. Related to this is the division between clergy and laity found in many churches, often leading to low participation of ordinary church members in ministry activities of the church. Furthermore, the lack of contextualization in religious practices and gospel communication strategies forms an impediment to being more missional in the Myanmar context. Finally, a missional approach is hampered by discipleship programs that center on individual spiritual growth, rather than outward-focused discipleship that aims for a spiritual transformation of the entire community.

We have seen how reconciliation with God is inherently linked to reconciliation with others by showing that it has both vertical and horizontal dimensions. We have learned that our identity as Christians supersedes national, ethnic, or cultural identities and fosters a welcoming community based on forgiveness and reconciliation. A missional church will be prepared to embrace reconciliation and acknowledge forgiveness as an integral part of discipleship and will commit to building inclusive communities where people from all ethnic and religious backgrounds feel welcome. In a society where a person's identity is shaped to a large extent by his or her ethnic affinity, Christians are called to build a community across ethnic boundaries. Christians in Myanmar will need to reflect on individual and communal attitudes and practices that may alienate people from other ethnicities, and implement ways to address these obstacles. They will consider ways to modify such praxes and introduce new ones contributing to more welcoming, inclusive Christian communities.

The inspiration for this book came from the observation that many churches in Myanmar struggle to effectively reach out to their surrounding communities, especially in multiethnic locations such as Yangon and other urban areas. While most churches thrive within their own ethnocultural communities, they often struggle to connect with the larger Buddhist-related population around them. This prompted an examination of the causes behind the Christian-Buddhist divide in Myanmar, the history of mission work in this country, and the biblical-theological foundations of a missional church.

My purpose was to explore a model for churches in Myanmar, in order that they may become more diverse and welcoming to various ethnicities in the country. This required rethinking the nature of the church and the need for reconciliation among the various ethnic groups within the Myanmar church. This internal reconciliation could lead toward forming more inclusive communities, where people from other ethnic and cultural backgrounds also feel welcome. We have seen how the present situation has developed from a combination of historical, political, and religious factors. We have considered the missiological, ecclesiological, and theological dynamics that have shaped and molded the church in Myanmar, followed by a theological reflection on the essence and mission of the church, particularly the implications for the church in a multicultural context. These observations formed the framework for a biblical-theological study of the nature of the church, its redemptive purpose in the world, and its calling to be a reconciling and unifying community. We have concluded that churches desiring to be missional should adopt a spiritual formation focus and embrace ethnic diversity, engaging the whole membership in contextualized ministry.

My hope is that this project will contribute to a flourishing of the church in Myanmar, inspiring and enabling God's people to show the reconciling power of the gospel and the multicolored nature of the body of Christ. The church in Myanmar has a long and rich history going back more than two hundred years. It is well established and recognized among the predominantly Christian minorities in the country. The next step would be for the church to expand beyond its traditional boundaries and become a community where people from all of Myanmar's ethnic groups can find a spiritual home. Christians are in a unique position to build bridges to each of Myanmar's ethnic communities, reaching out in forgiveness and love. If they are able to overcome their hurts and wounds, Christians could bring genuine reconciliation and become true peacemakers in this country, which has for so long been ravaged by conflict and animosity. In fact, with a Christian population of more than three million, the church in Myanmar may well play a major role in cross-cultural mission in the whole region, not only within Myanmar, but across national borders to neighboring Buddhist countries such as Thailand, Laos, and Cambodia. While each of these countries has its own history and traditions, they share a common heritage of Buddhism as the majority religion. As Myanmar churches become more missional among their own people groups, may they also awaken to their missionary calling across borders. With that missionary calling comes the responsibility and privilege to proclaim God's reconciling love, just as they themselves have received and experienced reconciliation with God and with one another.

Bibliography

Note: Most Burmese author names are listed without inversion of first name and family name, since in Myanmar there is no distinction between the two.

Beasley-Murray, George R. *John*. Word Biblical Commentary 36. Nashville, TN: Thomas Nelson, 1999. Olive Tree Bible Software.

Bischoff, Roger. *Buddhism in Myanmar: A Short History*. Kandi, Sri Lanka: Buddhist Publication Society, 1995.

Bosch, David J. *Transforming Mission: Paradigm Shifts in Theology of Mission*. 20th ed. Maryknoll, NY: Orbis, 2011.

Branson, Mark Lau, and Juan Francisco Martínez. *Churches, Cultures and Leadership: Practical Theology of Congregations and Ethnicities*. Downers Grove, IL: IVP Academic, 2011.

"Buddhism and State Power in Myanmar," International Crisis Group, Report 290, 5 September 2017, accessed 11 April 2022, https://www.crisisgroup.org/asia/south-east-asia/myanmar/290-buddhism-and-state-power-myanmar.

Burge, Gary M. *John*. NIV Application Commentary. Grand Rapids, MI: Zondervan, 2000.

Cady, John F. *A History of Modern Burma*. Ithaca, NY: Cornell University Press, 1958.

Campbell, Charlie. "Christian Chin 'Coerced to Buddhism by State.'" The Irrawaddy. 5 September 2012. Accessed 12 September 2017. http://www.irrawaddy.org/burma/christian-chin-coerced-to-buddhism-by-state.html.

Charney, Michael W. *A History of Modern Burma*. Cambridge: Cambridge University Press, 2008.

Cheesman, Nick. "How in Myanmar 'National Races' Came to Surpass Citizenship and Exclude Rohingya." *Journal of Contemporary Asia* 47, no. 3 (27 May 2017): 461–83. http://dx.doi.org/10.1080/00472336.2017.1297476.

Cho Cho Myaing. "Forgiveness toward National Reconciliation in Myanmar from Christian Perspective." MDiv diss., Myanmar Institute of Theology, 2013.

Cho, Patrick. "Helping Asian Churches Become Multi-Ethnic." In *Multi-Ethnic Churches*, edited by Jonathan Leeman, 65–68. 9Marks Journal IX. Washington DC: 9Marks, 2015.

Cin Do Kham. "Historical Values and Modes of Leadership in Myanmar: Assessment of Roots of Values among Christian Leaders in Yangon." PhD diss., Trinity International University, 1998.

Cockett, Richard. *Blood, Dreams and Gold: The Changing Face of Burma*. New Haven: Yale University Press, 2015.

Cope Suan Pau, Philip. "Peace Talk as Mission: Protestant Mission and Ethnic Insurgencies in Ethnocratic Buddhist Myanmar Today." Accessed 10 July 2017. https://www.academia.edu/19603279/Peace_Talk_as_Mission_Protestant_Mission_and_Ethnic_Insurgencies_in_Ethnocratic_Buddhist_Myanmar_Today.

Dawt Hlei Mawi. "A Comparative Study on the Development of Theological Institutes and Colleges Libraries in Yangon Division." MA diss., Myanmar Evangelical Graduate School of Theology, 2010.

DeYmaz, Mark. *Building a Healthy Multi-Ethnic Church: Mandate, Commitments and Practices of a Diverse Congregation.* San Francisco: Jossey-Bass, 2007.

Dunn, James D. G. *Romans 1–8.* Word Biblical Commentary 38a. Dallas: Word, 2012. Olive Tree Bible Software.

Easley, Kendell, and Christopher W. Morgan, eds. *The Community of Jesus: A Theology of the Church.* Nashville, TN: Broadman & Holman, 2013. Kindle.

Fleming, Rachel. *Hidden Plight: Christian Minorities in Myanmar.* United States Commission on International Religious Freedom, December 2016. Accessed 4 October 2017. https://www.uscirf.gov/sites/default/files/Hidden%20Plight.%20Christian%20Minorities%20in%20Burma.pdf.

Foulkes, Francis. *Ephesians.* Tyndale New Testament Commentaries 10. Downers Grove, IL: InterVarsity Press, 2008. Olive Tree Bible Study Digital Edition.

Ganzevoort, Ruaard. "Myanmar Experiences." Unpublished report. Kerk in Actie, 2011.

Goodman, Shona T. S. *From Princess to Persecuted: A Condensed History of the Shan/Tai to 1962.* N.p.: CreateSpace Independent Publishing Platform, 2014.

Gravers, Mikael, ed. *Exploring Ethnic Diversity in Burma.* 1st ed. NIAS Studies in Asian Topics. Copenhagen: Nordic Institute of Asian Studies, 2006.

Hesselgrave, David J., ed. *Missionshift: Global Mission Issues in the Third Millennium.* Nashville, TN: Broadman & Holman, 2010.

Hiebert, Paul G. *Anthropological Reflections on Missiological Issues.* Grand Rapids, MI: Baker, 1994.

International Commission of Jurists. *Challenges to Freedom of Religion or Belief in Myanmar: A Briefing Paper.* Geneva: International Commission of Jurists, October 2019.

Irons, Edward A. *Encyclopedia of Buddhism.* Encyclopedia of World Religions. New York: Infobase Publishing, 2006.

Jenkins, Philip. *The Next Christendom: The Coming of Global Christianity.* New York: Oxford University Press, 2002.

Jones, Lindsay. *Encyclopedia of Religion.* Vol. 9. 2nd ed. Farmington Hills, MI: Thomson-Gale, 2005.

Kam, C. Duh. "Christian Mission to Buddhists in Myanmar: A Study of Past, Present, and Future Approaches by Baptists." DMiss diss., United Theological Seminary, 1997.

Kanbawza Win. "The Beginning of the Christian Mission in Burma: 1519–1813." In *Christianity in Myanmar Conference,* edited by Kawlthangvuta and Johnny Maung

Latt. Unpublished conference papers. Bethany Theological Seminary, Yangon, Myanmar, 2002.

Kawl Thang Vuta. "A Brief History of the Planting and Growth of the Church in Burma." DMiss diss., Fuller Theological Seminary, 1983.

Keener, Craig S. *Romans*. New Covenant Commentary Series. Eugene, OR: Cascade, 2009.

Khai Chin Khua. "Dynamics of Renewal: A Historical Movement among the Zomi (Chin) in Myanmar." PhD diss., Fuller Theological Seminary, 1999.

Khai Za Dal. "An Investigation into the Barriers against Evangelization of Myanmar Buddhists from the Perspective of a Converted Myanmar Buddhist Monk and Implications for the Church in Myanmar." MA diss., Singapore Bible College, 1999.

Khin Mai Aung. "Why Myanmar Must Develop an Identity of Inclusion." Lion's Roar, 28 February 2019. Accessed 23 July 2019. https://www.lionsroar.com/commentary-why-myanmar-must-develop-an-identity-of-inclusion/.

Kraft, Charles H. *Anthropology for Christian Witness*. 2nd ed. Maryknoll, NY: Orbis, 1997.

Kruse, Colin. *John: An Introduction and Commentary*. Tyndale New Testament Commentaries 4. Nottingham: IVP Books, 2008. Olive Tree Bible Software.

Lal Tin Hre and Samuel Ngun Ling. "Select Surveys on Theological Education in Emerging Asian Churches: Myanmar." *Ecumenical Review* (WCC) 64, no. 2 (2012): 74–87.

Liana, Morris Remlal. "Developing Servant Leadership in the Wesleyan Church of Myanmar." DMin diss., Asbury Theological Seminary, 2004.

Mangalwadi, Vishal. *Truth and Transformation: A Manifesto for Ailing Nations*. Seattle: YWAM, 2009.

Marshall, Andrew. *The Trouser People: Burma in the Shadows of the Empire*. Bangkok: River Books, 2012.

Marshall, I. Howard. *Aspects of the Atonement: Cross and Resurrection in the Reconciling of God and Humanity*. Carlisle: Paternoster, 2007.

Maung Htin Aung. *Folk Elements in Burmese Buddhism*. Yangon: Religious Affairs Department, 1959.

Maung Maung. *Aung San of Burma*. 3rd ed. Yangon: Unity Publishing House, 2015.

Maung Maung Aye. "Spirit Belief in Burmese Buddhism: A Buddhist Perspective." *Engagement*, Judson Research Center Bulletin (Myanmar Institute of Theology) 7 (Dec. 2006): 46–51.

Maung Shwe Wa. *Burma Baptist Chronicle*. Edited by Genevieve Sowards and Erville Sowards. Rangoon: Burma Baptist Convention, 1963.

Mischke, Werner. *The Global Gospel: Achieving Missional Impact in Our Multicultural World*. Scottsdale, AZ: Mission ONE, 2015.

Mitton, C. Leslie. *Ephesians*. New Century Bible Commentary. Grand Rapids, MI: Eerdmans, 1989.

Nang Gin Khan. "Zomi Christianity and Cultural Transformation." PhD diss., Fuller Theological Seminary, 2010.

Naw, Angelene, and A. Naw. *Aung San and the Struggle for Burmese Independence.* Chiang Mai: University of Washington Press, 2002.

Newbigin, James Edward Lesslie. *The Gospel in a Pluralist Society.* Grand Rapids, MI: Eerdmans, 1989.

Ngun Ling, Samuel. *Christianity through Our Neighbors' Eyes: Rethinking the 200 Years Old American Baptist Missions in Myanmar.* Yangon: Judson Research Center, MIT, 2014.

———. *Communicating Christ in Myanmar: Issues, Interactions and Perspectives.* 3rd ed. Yangon: Judson Research Center, MIT, 2014.

———. "Doing Theology under the Bo Tree: Communicating the Christian Gospel in the Bama Buddhist Context." In *Called to Be a Community: Myanmar's in Search of New Pedagogies of Encounter; The First Seminar of Myanmar Theologians,* conference publication, edited by Samuel Ngun Ling, Than Win, and Peter Joseph, 171–84. Yangon: Association for Theological Education in Myanmar, 2003. Private circulation.

———. "Ethnicity, Religion and Theology in Asia: An Exploration from Myanmar Context." *Engagement,* Judson Research Center Bulletin (MIT) 7 (Dec 2006): 2–12.

Nyi Nyi Kyaw. "Myanmar's Rising Buddhist Nationalism: Impact on Foreign Investors." RSIS Commentaries. 15 May 2014. Accessed 6 November 2017. http://www.rsis. edu.sg/wp-content/uploads/2014/09/CO14090.pdf.

Osborne, Milton. *Southeast Asia: An Introductory History.* 9th ed. Crows Nest, Australia: Allen & Unwin, 2004.

Pedersen, Morten B. "Burma's Ethnic Minorities." *Critical Asian Studies* 40, no. 1 (2008): 45–66. http://search.ebscohost.com/login.aspx?direct=true&db=aph&A N=36570778&site=ehost-live.

Pe Maung Tin. "Certain Factors in the Buddhist-Christian Encounter." In *Called to Be a Community: Myanmar's in Search of New Pedagogies of Encounter; The First Seminar of Myanmar Theologians,* conference publication, edited by Samuel Ngun Ling, Than Win, and Peter Joseph, 90–99. Yangon: Association for Theological Education in Myanmar, 2003. Private circulation.

Poon, Michael Nai-Chiu. *Christian Movements in Southeast Asia: A Theological Exploration.* CSCA Christianity in Southeast Asia. Singapore: Genesis Books, 2010.

Puia. "Ethnic Diversities and Their Impacts on Today's Churches." MDiv diss., Myanmar Institute of Theology, 2015.

Pum Za Mang. "Separation of Church and State: A Case Study of Myanmar (Burma)." *Asia Journal of Theology* 25, no. 1 (2011): 42–58. http://search.ebscohost.com/ login.aspx?direct=true&db=aph&AN=59798731&site=ehost-live.

Pum Za Thang Tombing. "Training Zomi Christian Leaders for Missions to Hindus and Buddhists." DMin diss., Oral Roberts University, 2002.

The Republic of the Union of Myanmar. *The 2014 Myanmar Population and Housing Census – The Union Report: Religion; Census Report Volume 2-C.* Myanmar: Department of Population Ministry of Labour, Immigration and Population, July 2016. Accessed 7 November 2017. https://myanmar.unfpa.org/sites/default/files/pub-pdf/UNION_2C_Religion_EN.pdf.

Rowan, Peter A. "Proclaiming the Peacemaker: The Malaysian Church as an Agent of Reconciliation in a Multicultural Society." PhD diss., Open University, All Nations Christian College, 2010.

Salay Hta Oke. *Yangon Directory for Church and Christian Ministries.* Yangon: Christian Media Center, 2006.

Saw Gler Taw. "Factors Affecting the Growth of the Kayin Baptist Church with a View toward Facilitating Renewal." DMiss diss., Fuller Theological Seminary, 1996.

———. "A Renewal Strategy of the Karen Baptist Church of Myanmar (Burma) for Mission." ThM diss., Fuller Theological Seminary, 1992.

Saw Say Khu. "Assurance of Salvation." *Myanmar Pastor* (blog), 3 September 2007. Accessed 8 April 2018. http://myanmarpastor.blogspot.com/2007/09/assurance-of-salvation.html.

———. "Contextual Models for Church Growth in Myanmar." DMin diss., Union Theological Seminary Philippines & Myanmar Institute of Theology, 2007.

Schearf, Daniel. "Authorities Nurture Burma's Buddhist Chauvinism, Analysts Say." VOA News, 7 September 2012. Accessed 19 July 2017. https://www.voanews.com/a/burma_buddhist_chauvinism_nurtured_by_authorities/1503665.html.

Schreiter, Robert J. "Reconciliation as a Model of Mission." *New Theology Review* 10, no. 2 (1997), 11–12.

———. "Theology of Reconciliation and Peacemaking for Mission." 2003 Lectures for the British and Irish Association of Mission Studies, New College, University of Edinburgh, 23–25 June 2003. Accessed 19 June 2017. http://www.ehcounseling.com/materials/_applied_theology_of_reconciliation.pdf.

Sequeira, Aubrey. "Re-thinking Homogeneity: The Biblical Case for Multi-Ethnic Churches." In *Multi-ethnic Churches*, edited by Jonathan Leeman, 29–35. 9Marks Journal IX. Washington DC: 9Marks, 2015.

Shway Yoe (aka Sir James George Scott). *The Burman: His Life and Notions.* New York: Norton, 1963.

Spiro, Melford E. *Buddhism and Society: A Great Tradition and Its Burmese Vicissitudes.* 2nd ed. Berkeley: University of California Press, 1982.

———. *Burmese Supernaturalism.* Englewood Cliffs, NJ: Prentice-Hall, 1967.

Stetzer, Ed. "Laypeople and the Mission of God – Part 2: Reclaiming the Priesthood of All Believers." *MG Blog*, 30 July 2018. Accessed 14 April 2022. https://www.visionroom.com/laypeople-and-the-mission-of-god-part-2/.

Tegenfeldt, Aaron. "In Need of a Spiritual Framework for Peacebuilding: Burma and Beyond." MA diss., University of Victoria, 2004.

Thang Moe, David. "Being Church in the Midst of Pagodas." *Mission Studies: Journal of the International Association for Mission Studies* 31, no. 1 (2014): 22–43. http://search.ebscohost.com/login.aspx?direct=true&db=aph&AN=95625007&site=ehost-live.

Thant Myint-U. *The River of Lost Footsteps: A Personal History of Burma.* London: Faber & Faber, 2007.

———. *Where China Meets India: Burma and the New Crossroads of Asia.* New York: Farrar, Straus and Giroux, 2011.

Thein Nyunt, Peter. *Missions amidst Pagodas: Contextual Communication of the Gospel in Burmese Buddhist Context.* Yangon: Myint Offset, 2012.

Tint Lwin. "Contextualization of the Gospel: An Effective Strategy for the Evangelization of the Theravada Buddhists in Myanmar." PhD diss., Southern Baptist Theological Seminary, 1997.

Torres, Hazel. "Christians Being Pushed out of Their Own Church by Buddhist Monks in Myanmar." *Christianity Today.* Last modified 8 May 2016. Accessed 7 November 2017. https://www.christiantoday.com/article/christians.being.pushed.out.of.their.own.church.by.buddhist.monks.in.myanmar/85599.htm.

Tuscangate, Kosak. "Burmese Neo-Nazi Movement Rising against Muslims." The Irrawaddy. 24 March 2013. Accessed 6 November 2017. https://www.irrawaddy.com/opinion/guest-column/burmese-neo-nazi-movement-rising-against-muslims.html.

U Hla Bu. "The Christian Encounter with Buddhism in Burma." *International Review of Mission* 47, no. 186 (1958): 171–77.

Unrepresented Nations and Peoples Organization. "Chin: New Report Sheds Light on Religious Discrimination." 10 September 2012. Accessed 6 November 2017. http://www.unpo.org/article/14830.

Van Dorp, Arend. "Developing Missional Churches in the Myanmar Context." TM751 Term Paper, Fuller Theological Seminary, 2015.

Van Essen, Jelle P. "Recognizing Reconciliation: The Role of Culture on Post World War II and Post-Cold War Reconciliatory Processes and Acts of Apology." MA diss., Erasmus University, 2014.

Van Gelder, Craig. *The Essence of the Church: A Community Created by the Spirit.* Grand Rapids, MI: Baker, 2000.

Van Ram Oke. "Missioners as Contextualizers: The Theology and Practice of Contextualization in the Ministry of Bread of Life to the Bama Community of New Dagon City." DMin diss., Asia Graduate School of Theology, 2007.

Van Rheenen, Gailyn. "Contrasting Missional and Church Growth Perspectives." *Missiology.com* blog, MR #34. 17 January 2011. Accessed 6 July 2018. http://www.missiology.org/blog/GVR-MR-34-Contrasting-Missional-and-Church-Growth-Perspectives.

Volf, Miroslav. *Exclusion and Embrace: A Theological Exploration of Identity, Otherness, and Reconciliation.* Nashville, TN: Abingdon Press, 2010.

———. "The Social Meaning of Reconciliation." *Occasional Papers on Religion in Eastern Europe* 18, no. 3 (1998). Accessed 21 October 2017. http://digitalcommons. georgefox.edu/ree/vol18/iss3/3.

Walton, Matthew J. "The 'Wages of Burman-Ness': Ethnicity and Burman Privilege in Contemporary Myanmar," *Journal of Contemporary Asia* 43, no. 1 (2013): 1–27. Accessed 24 July 2019. https://www.tandfonline.com/doi/full/10.1080/0047233 6.2012.730892.

Walton, Matthew J., and Susan Hayward. *Contesting Buddhist Narratives: Democratization, Nationalism, and Communal Violence in Myanmar.* Policy Studies 71. Honolulu: East-West Center, 2014.

Wikipedia. "Myanmar Institute of Theology." Accessed 19 October 2017. https:// en.wikipedia.org/wiki/Myanmar_Institute_of_Theology.

Willard, Dallas. *The Divine Conspiracy: Rediscovering Our Hidden Life in God.* San Francisco: HarperCollins, 1998.

Williams, Jarvis J. "Racial Reconciliation, the Gospel, and the Church." In *Multi-Ethnic Churches*, edited by Jonathan Leeman, 8–12. 9Marks Journal IX. Washington DC: 9Marks, 2015.

Woodward, J. R. *Creating a Missional Culture: Equipping the Church for the Sake of the World.* Downers Grove, IL: InterVarsity Press, 2013.

Wright, Christopher J. H. *The Mission of God's People: A Biblical Theology of the Church's Mission.* Biblical Theology for Life. Grand Rapids, MI: Zondervan, 2010.

Wu, Jackson. "How Do Evangelicals Define 'Contextualization'?" Jackson Wu, 24 May 2013. Accessed 18 July 2015. http://jacksonwu.org/2013/05/24/how-do-evangelicasl-define-contextualization/.

———. *One Gospel for All Nations.* Pasadena, CA: William Carey Library, 2015.

Yen Saning. "Mother-Tongue Instruction Pushed for Burma's Schools." The Irrawaddy, 4 February 2014. https://www.irrawaddy.com/news/burma/mother-tongue-instruction-pushed-burmas-schools.html.

Zam Khat Kham. "Burmese Nationalism and Christianity in Myanmar: Christian Identity and Witness in Myanmar Today." PhD diss., Concordia Seminary, 2015. Accessed 7 November 2017. http://scholar.csl.edu/phd/22.

Index

🌐 Langham™
PARTNERSHIP

Langham Literature and its imprints are a ministry of Langham Partnership.

Langham Partnership is a global fellowship working in pursuit of the vision God entrusted to its founder John Stott –

> *to facilitate the growth of the church in maturity and Christ-likeness through raising the standards of biblical preaching and teaching.*

Our vision is to see churches in the Majority World equipped for mission and growing to maturity in Christ through the ministry of pastors and leaders who believe, teach and live by the word of God.

Our mission is to strengthen the ministry of the word of God through:
- nurturing national movements for biblical preaching
- fostering the creation and distribution of evangelical literature
- enhancing evangelical theological education

especially in countries where churches are under-resourced.

Our ministry

Langham Preaching partners with national leaders to nurture indigenous biblical preaching movements for pastors and lay preachers all around the world. With the support of a team of trainers from many countries, a multi-level programme of seminars provides practical training, and is followed by a programme for training local facilitators. Local preachers' groups and national and regional networks ensure continuity and ongoing development, seeking to build vigorous movements committed to Bible exposition.

Langham Literature provides Majority World preachers, scholars and seminary libraries with evangelical books and electronic resources through publishing and distribution, grants and discounts. The programme also fosters the creation of indigenous evangelical books in many languages, through writer's grants, strengthening local evangelical publishing houses, and investment in major regional literature projects, such as one volume Bible commentaries like *The Africa Bible Commentary* and *The South Asia Bible Commentary*.

Langham Scholars provides financial support for evangelical doctoral students from the Majority World so that, when they return home, they may train pastors and other Christian leaders with sound, biblical and theological teaching. This programme equips those who equip others. Langham Scholars also works in partnership with Majority World seminaries in strengthening evangelical theological education. A growing number of Langham Scholars study in high quality doctoral programmes in the Majority World itself. As well as teaching the next generation of pastors, graduated Langham Scholars exercise significant influence through their writing and leadership.

To learn more about Langham Partnership and the work we do visit **langham.org**

www.ingramcontent.com/pod-product-compliance
Lightning Source LLC
Chambersburg PA
CBHW072201090426
42740CB00012B/2342